The Ancient World: Source Books

General Editor: Peter Walcot
Professor of Classics, University of Cardiff

The Individual
and the State

Edited with an Introduction by

H. MacL. CURRIE
Senior Lecturer in Classics, Queen Mary College,
University of London

Dent, London
Hakkert, Toronto

© Introduction, translations and commentary,
J. M. Dent & Sons Ltd, 1973

Made in Great Britain
at the
Aldine Press · Letchworth · Herts
for
J. M. DENT & SONS LTD
Aldine House · Albemarle Street · London
First published in 1973

Published in Canada, the United States of
America and its dependencies by A. M. HAKKERT
LTD, 554 Spadina Crescent, Toronto M5s
2J9, Canada

This book if bound as a paperback is
subject to the condition that it may not
be issued on loan or otherwise except in
its original binding

This book is set in
9 on 10 and 10 on 11 point Baskerville 169

Dent edition
Hardback ISBN 0 460 10150 1
Paperback ISBN 0 460 11150 7

Hakkert edition
Hardback ISBN 0 88866 529 6
Paperback ISBN 0 88866 530 x

Library of Congress Catalog
Card No. 73 82993

Foreword

Although few today study Greek and Latin at school or college, there has never been a more widespread interest in classical civilisation and culture. How academically respectable is such an interest unless it is reinforced by an ability to read the Greek and Latin languages? Certainly it is crucially important that a student should have a direct contact with the primary evidence, that is, the evidence offered by what our ancient authorities say themselves. Yet this need may be met by the provision of sound translations, for these can go a long way towards supplying an acceptable alternative to an actual knowledge of Greek and Latin. It is no longer possible to argue, as it was possible in antiquity, that a man can attain mastery of all branches of learning; the sheer complexity of the modern world forces us to be selective in education as in so much else. It is not reasonable to expect the student to be conversant with a variety of languages, but it would be absurd if we restricted our studies to the exclusive consideration of those speaking and writing our native tongue. In fact, if an effort to guide a student's interest is to be really constructive, we are obliged to do more than just supply adequate translations; we must also be willing to collect together as representative a selection of the relevant evidence in translation as is possible. What then is left to the student? A great deal. Questions are posed and evidence is presented, but the student finds the answers himself. The student must think for himself, and his thoughts will not be casual or ill-founded if he and his colleagues can and do make frequent reference to the primary evidence which it is the purpose of this series of source-books to collect and to translate.

PETER WALCOT

Contents

IV. THE INDIVIDUAL AND THE STATE: TENSIONS

V. WOMEN AND THE STATE

Preface

The interlocking civilisations of Greece and Rome, though exercising a powerful and pervasive influence on the growth and pattern of subsequent Western European culture, were nevertheless founded upon many attitudes and prepossessions different from ours today. But this fact does not prevent us from learning much about our own condition through the study of this particular area of the past, conveniently self-contained as it is. Between the ancients and ourselves there are a considerable number of problems in common, not the least of which is that of the individual within the community of the state, and the theoretical and practical responses of antiquity to these have great instructional importance for us today.

The basis of ancient society, Greek and Roman, was the family group, all the members of which were descended from a common ancestry and thus related by blood. This extended family, comprehending a wide circle of people, stands in sharp contrast to the very restricted conception of the family to which Western man has become used. The system of clans, with their various alliances and inter-relationships, played a notable part in the evolution of society and political life at both Athens and Rome.

And then there is *areté* (which we, inadequately, render 'virtue' or 'excellence'). In fifth-century Athens this word had come principally to refer to those qualities which make for success. Values were in a state of flux as a result of the probings of thinkers who could find no objective foundation for knowledge and for such notions as justice. Might, it was declared, was Right (see p. 59 ff.). For very many people 'virtue' was devoid of moral content. With Socrates, Plato and, after them, Aristotle there is a sustained effort to assert the prime significance of the co-operative qualities which are to be ranged under the heading of justice; they preached a richer and more generous gospel, and for them excellence in the art of living involved strongly a sense of social obligations (for Aristotle on *areté* see comments on p. 34 f.).

In their writings and speculation on social and political questions Plato and Aristotle place their stress on the proper development of character in each member of the community. Plato's approach is poetic, enthusiastic, visionary. His exuberant style speaks of his large imaginings and hopes for man as a political creature. He writes with a confident dogmatism, laying down in *ex cathedra* fashion his schemes for the organisation of society; but despite all this and the elaborate metaphysical framework, his ultimate aim was not really to convince but to convert—to inspire people with a vision of a new order of society, to instil into them a yearning for a different kind of world in which justice prevails. Ordinary experience shows that his analogy between the individual and the state (for which see p. 66 ff.) is not justified; but that is not the point: it forms part of his wider ideal—to encourage the growth of human personality to its appropriate fulfilment in accordance with the best possible moral standards.

Aristotle in his contribution to the great Greek debate concerning the aim of life was more direct and down to earth. Observation of actual practice and hard-headed reasoning form the staple of his argument, but he still with Plato sees human character and the need to train it as the key to the political problem.

The Romans, having codified very early in their history the laws of their nation, fashioned for themselves a flexible constitution. Little given to theorising, they had a kind of 'horse sense' which guided them in their affairs, as well as, in general, a strongly conformist attitude. Later, when they discovered Greek philosophy in the second century B.C., the work of applying its lessons to the Roman situation began.

Both civilisations were built upon slavery. The essence of the Greek state was that it was the state of a class, being the possession of those who had the freedom to serve it, though the state remained greater than its rulers. Rome, with its instinct for order, gained and, for centuries, controlled a vast empire, thus providing for posterity an impressive example of administrative efficiency and planning.

Differences of outlook exist between the ancients and ourselves, but their highest ideals have affected us and can continue to do so if we take the trouble to study them. In considering some of the ways in which the ancient Greeks and Romans thought about the relationship of the individual and the state, we are penetrating below the surface to an important sector of their communal life, and in the process we are led to see more clearly into our own position.

This book contains, after a general historical introduction, five chapters, each dealing with a major section of the subject; and in each chapter there is a number of sub-sections consisting of translated passages from classical authors exemplifying the particular theme, along with explanatory material and some comments for discussion either in seminar classes or essays (or in both).

I am very grateful to the General Editor of the series, Professor Peter Walcot, for scholarly help and encouragement. The faults that remain are my own.

H. MacL. Currie

September 1973

Select Bibliography

A useful work of general reference is the *Oxford Classical Dictionary* (revised, 1970, under the editorship of N. G. L. Hammond and H. H. Scullard). Translations grow in number; the most comprehensive series is the *Loeb Classical Library* (Harvard: London, Heinemann), and many important works are now available in Everyman and Penguin translations. The editions given below are the latest.

THE GREEKS

Adkins, A. W. H. *Merit and Responsibility: a Study in Greek Values* (Oxford, 1960).

Allan, D. J. *The Philosophy of Aristotle* (Oxford, 1970).

Andrewes, A. *Greek Society* (Pelican, 1971).

Barker, E. *Greek Political Theory* (Methuen, 1960).

Barker, E. *The Political Thought of Plato and Aristotle* (Dover, 1959).

Bonner, R. J., and Smith, G. *The Administration of Justice from Homer to Aristotle* (2 vols, Greenwood, 1969).

Bowra, C. M. *The Greek Experience* (Weidenfeld and Nicolson, 1960; Mentor, 1967).

Brunt, P. A. (on Thucydides). Introduction to an abridged translation in the series 'The Great Histories' (New York, Washington Square Press, 1963).

Burn, A. R. *History of Greece* (Pelican, 1970).

Dodds, E. R. *The Greeks and the Irrational* (University of California, 1951).

Ehrenberg, V. *The Greek State* (Methuen, 1969; Norton, 1964).

Field, G. C. *Plato and His Contemporaries* (Methuen, 1967; Barnes and Noble, 1967).

Finley, J. H. *Thucydides* (University of Michigan, 1963).

Finley, M. I. (ed.) *Slavery in Classical Antiquity* (Heffer, 1960; Barnes and Noble, 1968).

Finley, M. I. *The Ancient Greeks* (Pelican, 1971; Viking Press, 1963).

Grube, G. M. A. *Plato's Thought* (Methuen, 1970; Beacon Press, 1958).

Guthrie, W. K. C. *The Sophists* (Cambridge, 1971).

Hammond, N. G. L. *History of Greece to 322 B.C.* (Oxford, 1967).

Huxley, G. L. *Early Sparta* (Faber, 1962; Barnes and Noble, 1971).

Jaeger, W. *Aristotle* (English translation, Oxford, 1962).

Jaeger, W. *Paedeia: The Ideals of Greek Culture* (3 vols; English translation, Oxford, 1965).

Lacey, W. K. *The Family in Classical Greece* (Thames and Hudson, 1968; Cornell University, 1968).

Larsen, J. A. O. *Greek Federal States: Their Institutions and History* (Oxford, 1968).

Lloyd-Jones, H. (ed.) *The Greek World* (Pelican, 1962).

Marrou, H. I. *A History of Education in Antiquity* (English translation, New American Library, 1969).

Michell, H. *Sparta* (Heffer, Cambridge, 1952).

Nilsson, M. *Greek Popular Religion* (New York, Columbia, 1940).

Randall, J. H. *Aristotle* (New York, Columbia, 1963).

Tarn, W. W., and Griffiths, G. T. *Hellenistic Civilization* (Methuen, 1966; St Martin, 1952).

Taylor, A. E. *Plato, the Man and his Work* (Methuen, 1966; Barnes and Noble, 1966).

Welles, C. B. *Alexander and the Hellenistic World* (Hakkert), 1970).

THE ROMANS

Adcock, F. E. *Roman Political Ideas and Practice* (Ann Arbor, 1959).

Altheim, F. *Roman Religion* (Methuen, 1938).

Balsdon, J. P. V. D. *Life and Leisure in Ancient Rome* (Bodley Head, 1969; McGraw, 1969).

Balsdon, J. P. V. D. *Rome: the Story of an Empire* (Weidenfeld and Nicolson, 1971).

Balsdon, J. P. V. D. *The Romans* (Watts, 1965; Basic, 1966).

Boak, A. E. R. *A History of Rome* (Macmillan, New York, 1965).

Cary, M. *History of Rome* (Macmillan, 1954; St Martin, 1954).

Cary, M., and Haarhoff, T. J. *Life and Thought in the Greek and Roman World* (Methuen, 1940; Barnes and Noble, 1959).

Charlesworth, M. P. *The Roman Empire* (Oxford, 1951).

Fowler, W. Warde. *Rome* (Oxford, 1967).

Fowler, W. Warde. *Social Life at Rome in the Age of Cicero* (Macmillan, 1963).

Frank, T. *Some Aspects of Social Behaviour in Ancient Rome* (Cooper Square, 1969).

Grant, M. *The World of Rome* (Mentor, 1967).

Scullard, H. H. *From the Gracchi to Nero* (Methuen, 1970; Barnes and Noble, 1970).

Starr, C. G. *Civilization and the Caesars* (Norton, 1965).

Stobart, J. C. *The Grandeur that was Rome* (Sidgwick and Jackson, 1971; Praeger, 1969).

Taylor, L. R. *Party Politics in the Age of Caesar* (University of California, 1949).

Part One

Introduction

THE INDIVIDUAL AND SOCIETY

The Latin term *individuum* is a rendering of the Greek *atomon*, and so means 'that which cannot be cut or divided'. Cicero uses the word in this way, as does Seneca. By later antiquity the meaning of 'a single thing, alone of its kind, distinct from others', 'a unique thing', had become established.

The philosophers define a person as an individual which is conscious of itself in relation to universal being. The definition of Boethius which runs 'a person is an individual substantiation of rationality' was standard throughout the Middle Ages. But if, with medieval thinkers, we believe that it is only through our reason that we can apprehend the universal, then it does not matter greatly whether we employ rationality or universality in our definition.

For its existence and development personality requires community, though not all forms of community are equally conducive to its growth; personality can arise only in communities in which the universal is present at least potentially. Amongst animals which live gregariously (wolves, deer, elephants), for instance, there is doubtless to some extent a sense of community, but because they possess no conception of universal bearing and significance for their individual lives, the individuals are not persons. The relationship of the individual person to the universal community is one of the crucial issues in the study of human history.

In this book we shall be considering, with the aid of illustrative passages in translation, important aspects of the classical Greek and Roman attitudes to the individual and the state—attitudes which in both cultures underwent change and

variation. But first let us look, in brief survey, at the progress
of this debate in subsequent history.

Historically, a cyclic tendency is discernible in human
society, in which the emphasis moves from a general order to
the individual, and then from the individual back to a general
order. In the earliest stages of social organisation the individual
merely forms part of an economy by whose conventions and
rules he is severely restricted. With the growth of civilisation
there comes division of labour, which enhances the status of the
individual, giving him a measure of independence and in time
making him impatient of authority. He becomes more self-
reliant and unwilling to accept anything not in keeping with
his own opinions and ideas, a situation marking the start of the
dissolution of social stability and community life. A reaction
therefore comes about leading to fresh assertions of authority.
In the study of a society and its historical development we
shall be alert to the alternating influence of the individual
and of a transcendent general order on the determination of
events.

In the Middle Ages (whose starting point we may conveniently take as the fall of the Western Roman Empire in
A.D. 476) Christian and Roman conceptions had combined to
create belief in the unity of mankind under a universal law of
nature. Generalisations with regard to this period of a thousand
years are particularly difficult and dangerous, but an important
characteristic of social and political life was the joint influence
of convention and the Church.

In sixteenth-century Europe the spread of Protestantism
broke down the old order of things. Martin Luther (1483–
1546) had provided the emotional instigation for the movement, while John Calvin (1509–1564) was its intellectual
leader, giving the first reasoned definition and justification of
it in his 'Institutions of the Christian Religion'. The essence of
Protestantism is the acceptance by the individual Christian of
his direct responsibility to God rather than to the Church.
Traditional doctrine saw the Church as a visible and continuous spiritual society with strong juridical and disciplinary
powers for members' correction and guidance. Protestant
individualism repudiates the idea of the Church as a uniform

institution with monitorial functions. It is on the question of Church-order that the movement for Christian unity today experiences its most acute difficulties; to reconcile within one generally acceptable formula the two widely differing views of what is the essence of the Church stands out as the primary matter for resolution by ecclesiastical leaders. To put the issue briefly, we could say that while the older doctrine sees the relationship between the Church and its outward form as that between a man and his body, the later teaching sees it as that between a man and his clothes.

Apart from the strictly ecclesiastical sphere, perhaps Calvinism's greatest influence arose from the emphasis by Calvin himself upon hard work as a divinely enjoined duty. This emphasis changed the medieval ideas about the blessedness of poverty and the wrongfulness of usury. Calvinism preached against luxury and encouraged frugality; commercial success was taken as a certain indication of God's approval. In this way Calvinism was related to the rise of capitalism, but whether as cause or effect scholars disagree. Max Weber, the German sociologist, maintained that Calvinism provided a powerful incentive at least for the rise of capitalism or was even its cause; but the opposite viewpoint has been advanced by Marx, Sombart and Richard Tawney, who have argued that Calvinism itself actually was a result of developing capitalism, providing it with an ideological justification.

Whatever the truth, a competitive individualism strongly associated with commercialism arose in the sixteenth century. In no centuries has a 'sturdy individualism' been more vigorously proclaimed than in the seventeenth and eighteenth, and by no philosophers more energetically than by Descartes and Locke. Yet in the eighteenth century this same individualism came under attack from the formidable David Hume, and under an onslaught at once philosophical, cultural and economic, it died in the nineteenth century. And so today political thought for the most part has been communal in its emphasis. The two opposed political and social ideologies of Communism and Fascism, which have their roots in nineteenth-century theorising, have during this century uncompromisingly asserted the supremacy of the state. Communism advocates the common possession of property in a state and the organisation of civil life on the principle 'from each according to his ability, to each according to his needs'. Modern states which have embarked on a communist course are Russia, China and Cuba. Fascism is a totalitarian system standing for the negation of all the liberal ideals which have gradually evolved over the past five hundred years in the West. Under it private enterprise is encouraged and protected, though there is close state control. In Italy Benito Mussolini set up an absolutist government in 1922 and ruled for twenty-one years. Adolf Hitler in Germany and Francisco Franco in Spain followed suit, while in Japan a militaristic clique of similar outlook obtained power. In the Second World War (1939–1945) Britain and the Commonwealth, along with the U.S.S.R. and the U.S.A., were engaged in a struggle unparalleled for its ferocity and scale in human history against the combined might of Germany, Italy, Japan and their satellites.

Democracy as we know it owes much to Protestantism. Luther believed that all religious authority proceeds from God alone and does not lie with prelates, and he held that in religion all men are equal. Politically, however, he strongly upheld the authority of the princes of the day, rejecting democracy as a form of government. Even so, his religious ideas had their political effects and application. There was a long series of bitterly fought wars between Reformers and adherents of Rome, but finally the contenders realised that the only answer to the problem was to cultivate tolerance and to try to co-exist peacefully. From this beginning there arose and spread a greater open-mindedness and recognition of that political individualism which belongs to democracy. Also, some Protestant churches were by their constitution self-governing, which resulted in a flow of trained people for participation in democratic processes.

In England the Petition of Rights was passed by Parliament (1628) in order to vindicate the citizens' ancient liberties against the high-handed actions of Charles I. Grievances still remained, however, and the Puritan Revolution during the 1640's marks a further step in the direction of greater freedom in religious and political matters. In 1689, after the so-called Glorious Revolution, there was passed the Bill of Rights, model of the many similar charters of later times in other countries (the U.S.A. included), which put its stress upon individual freedom in government, law and religion. It definitively laid down, too, the principle that political authority rests with Parliament and not the sovereign. But aristocratic, not democratic, government was its immediate result. Wealth and noble birth were the way to political influence and power in Britain during the eighteenth and nineteenth centuries. It was in fact only during the latter century that the term democracy and the idea it represents began to have currency amongst English-speaking people.

Looking back over European history since the Middle Ages, a period in which have occurred the Renaissance, the Reformation, the rise of capitalism, the Industrial Revolution and the struggle for democracy, we notice that certain values and ideals have gradually matured and grown into acceptance (not at the same rate in all places and certainly not without various obstacles and reverses). The essential dignity and sanctity of human life, freedom of thought and criticism, faith in human progress and in the power of reason, religious and political tolerance, popular government (those who govern being answerable for their actions to the governed), the rule of law based on the impartial administration of justice, the necessity of education for all and of peace amongst nations—these are some of the things we have learned to esteem highly. But to the radical temper the usual democratic procedures often seem to be just pedantic formalities retarding or obstructing such reforms as may be considered still necessary. A knowledge of history, however, should bestow a sense of proportion. We have succeeded in establishing a definite place for the indvidual in society and assigning a distinct value to him. There is a danger that hasty action carried out in his name and for his good may actually in the long run be to his disadvantage.

THE GREEK SITUATION

The *polis* or city-state was for centuries the context for Greek
life and thought. Happiness (*eudaemonia*) according to both
statesmen and philosophers lay in the loyal fulfilment of civic
duty. The city-state was regarded as the ideal social organism
for the proper realisation of the good life; philosophical discussion on ethical questions started from the presupposition
that the life of a free citizen in a Greek *polis* was the only kind of
existence worthy of a man. Socrates under sentence of death in
the prison at Athens refused his friends' offer of help to escape
on the grounds that the laws of the *polis* must be obeyed even
though he had been undeservedly condemned under them:
just as a son ought not to strike his elderly parent, so the citizen
ought not to violate the laws of the state which has nurtured
and protected him (see the extract from Plato's *Crito* for the
argument, p. 102 ff.).

The usual political development of a classical Greek state to
about 500 B.C. was as follows: monarchy—aristocracy—
tyranny (dictatorship)—oligarchy or moderate democracy—
radical democracy (*demokratia*). The rate of development varied
in different places. Some states remained monarchies or
aristocracies till the end of the classical age in the fourth century B.C. Not infrequently there were cases of reversion from
radical democracy to oligarchy or dictatorship.

Monarchy gave way at an early date to aristocratic government. When the Greek-speaking tribes had settled in the areas
which they conquered, the former need for strong leaders
became less. Acquiring big estates, nobles gradually grew
independent of the kings. By about 700 B.C. the principal noble
families in the majority of advanced states had by joint action
deposed their kings and assumed power themselves. The royal
functions were entrusted to one or more magistrates appointed
by the nobles or elected by the assembly from a number of
aristocratic candidates.

This kind of government was in turn overthrown during
the seventh and sixth centuries B.C. by tyrants—despots whose
rule, though not necessarily tyrannical in our sense, and
sometimes in fact moderate and enlightened, was nevertheless

unconstitutional and autocratic. The rise of the tyrant was due to the discontent of the unprivileged masses aggrieved by the oppressive misrule of the aristocratic clique. Usually he came to the fore as the professed champion of the people, being either a noble himself, commanding popular support against the rest of his class, or an hereditary king who had made himself absolute, or a military adventurer who had seized and retained power by force, or a magistrate who held on to office after the expiry of his term. Tyrannies did not tend to last long, but they were attended by certain real benefits. They prepared the way for democracy by humbling the pride of the nobles and bringing their destructive feuds under control. Public works, too, giving employment to the poor at the expense of the wealthy, were a mark of tyrannies, whose policy was to subdue the rich and powerful. Art and literature were greatly encouraged to counteract political restlessness, and closer relations with foreign powers were cultivated, which resulted in the growth of trade and the development of wider contacts between Greeks and barbarians.

But rule responsible to no one could not have an indefinite appeal. In time the conception of equality before the laws for all citizens began to develop, though the individual citizen's entitlement to political privileges was related to his financial status—a man's influence and position in the community had to depend upon what contribution he made to its maintenance and protection. The richest citizens in classical Greek states usually in fact bore the heaviest burden in the performance of civic duties and in the battle-line itself. During the early classical period the phalanx of heavily armed infantrymen became tactically of greater importance than cavalry or chariots, and this made the 'middle class', who provided the infantry, more important than the aristocracy, from which had come the cavalry and charioteers.

In the course of the fifth century radical democracy (*demokratia*) steadily advanced, mainly in those states where sailors, artisans and small traders had become numerous. Under *demokratia* it was common for all citizens to be accorded political privileges (including the right to hold political offices) without reference to their financial status. In some

democratic states poorer citizens received public grants, so
that they could undertake civic offices. The state's policy was
directly controlled by the citizens' assembly, votes being taken
on all important questions. Those who had the greatest persuasive capacity tended to become the leaders of the state,
which meant that the citizen body sometimes fell victim to the
glib oratory of unscrupulous speakers who played on their
emotions and prejudices, whipping up on occasion mass
hysteria. Minorities, too, which had formerly wielded influence
sometimes suffered oppression because of class-hatred that was
fomented. Slaves and resident aliens, even in the most advanced Greek democracies, had no civic rights at all, though
they formed a large part of the populace. And women were
denied any right to vote, hold any public office (except perhaps
a religious one) or speak in the assembly.

The city-state in origin goes back to the time of Homer and
Hesiod when the old monarchical system was fading out. The
Homeric epics, the *Iliad* and the *Odyssey*, were composed in the
eighth century B.C., but though they are set in a remote past,
without doubt they reflect the contemporary social order. The
Homeric world has two strata—that of the great people, and a
lower one which comes to our attention in the similes and in the
persons of servants. The independent landowner is the most
important figure, though a few craftsmen and professional men
(smiths, carpenters, potters, itinerant doctors and minstrels)
have achieved independent status. Homeric society and medieval chivalry may at first sight appear similar, but in Homer
farming bulks very large as an occupation. Everyone is close to
the land. The word *polis* in Homer signifies no more than a
fortified site or town without any of the later political connota-
tions. This closeness to the land was to be an abiding feature of
Greek civilisation and the Greek economy for centuries. (And
since, we may note in passing, towns remained relatively few
in number and small in size, and since most people were on the
land, Greeks could not be aware of the country as a special,
separate thing. Hence 'appreciation of Nature' and 'nature
poetry' did not exist in antiquity till really huge cities like
Alexandria, founded in 323 B.C. by Alexander the Great and
named after him, arose.) The general agrarian atmosphere in

Homer is instanced by the challenge to a mowing and ploughing match which Odysseus issues to the suitor Eurymachus
(*Odyssey* 18. 365 ff.), and by the depiction on Achilles' shield
of a squire or landowner standing contentedly amongst his
harvesters (*Iliad* 18. 550 ff.).

In the Homeric *polis* we find king and subjects sharing in its
defence. A very close connection remained throughout classical Greek history between the ability to bear arms and
citizenship. City-states, oligarchic and democratic alike,
exercised the strictest control over admission to citizenship, and
how exactly citizenship was to be defined was one of the problems that continued to exercise political thinkers.

The *Odyssey* gives us more and greater glimpses of ordinary
life than the *Iliad*, and it also probes deeper into moral and
religious questions; the problem of conduct and that of individual responsibility begin now to be raised, and we start to
have intimations of those problems of justice (*diké*) of which we
are to hear much in Hesiod and which are to become a chief
preoccupation of Greek thought.

In Homer the action and interest are largely engrossed by
the heroic monarchs. For Hesiod, whose poems are perhaps to
be dated round about 700 B.C. and who belonged to the class of
small farmers, the kings are not, in Homeric phrase, 'sons of
Zeus' but 'devourers of the people'. His *Works and Days*,
addressed to his brother Perses who, having squandered his
share of the patrimony, tried by bribing the local authorities to
get Hesiod's as well, is a didactic poem in which the farmer's
year in Boeotia (where he lived) is described. The poet's
unjust treatment at the hands of aristocratic owners is one
major theme, closely connected with which is the struggle in
his mind between a pessimistic view of things and a deep
belief in the existence of justice as an absolute, universal principle. Hesiod's general outlook is that of a peasant; he bemoans
the bad conditions that prevail, but he has no political solution
to offer. His answer to the contemporary ills is to insist that
those in power ought to practise justice and thereby win the
approval of Zeus, while the lower orders ought to devote
themselves to hard work. A note of protest against oppression
of the poor by the rich is clearly sounded in Hesiod.

Oppression was something with which Solon had to deal when in 594 B.C. he was empowered by his fellow citizens to devise remedies to bring civil strife at Athens to an end. There was great need of political and economic reforms. The nobles (*Eupatridae*) possessed nearly all the land, and the poor lacked any political voice or influence. Enslavement for debt was common. As a first step Solon cancelled all debts and mortgages, setting free those who had been enslaved as a result of defaulting on repayments to creditors, and he brought in legislation making such enslavement illegal. He promoted the growth of Athenian industry and trade, and he encouraged olive culture in Attica. He graded the free citizens into four classes, the criterion for political eligibility being income. Solon set forth his political and ethical ideas in verse, and was honoured as the first Athenian poet. Traditionally, too, he is one of the Seven Sages of antiquity. With him the individual free citizen is beginning to come into focus against the background of the state.

Meanwhile, in the personal or solo lyric poetry of Sappho and her contemporary Alcaeus explicitly private themes and concerns were being treated. Both, writing round about the end of the seventh century B.C. and the beginning of the sixth, were natives of the island of Lesbos. Sappho sings about herself and her friends; Alcaeus led a busy and convivial life, waging a long, brave fight against the Lesbian tyrants, Pittacus and Myrtilus, and his poetry mirrors his diverse interests and activity. Alcaeus invented the celebrated figure of the Ship of State.

Sparta reproduced the picture painted in Homer more than any other part of Greece. A purely martial community, it was, like Prussia, 'not a country which had an army, but an army which had a country'. There were only a few thousand Spartans, greatly outnumbered by the original inhabitants of the country whom they had conquered and enslaved, and so they kept themselves in a constant state of soldierly readiness in case of revolt, doing no normal work at all and living off their subjects. They could not survive and retain authority without submitting to the most rigorous military discipline, totally surrendering their wills to the state, and practising above all courage and self-sacrifice. Faced with the sometimes anarchic democracy and individualism of Athens, Plato and Aristotle looked on this system with admiration, though in fact it was too severe and fitted only for an under-developed nation—hence its failure as the Spartans' political horizon grew.

In the early years of the fifth century B.C. Athens took the lead in Greek opposition to Persian aggrandisement. The Persians received a notable setback at the battle of Marathon (490 B.C.), and were decisively defeated at Salamis ten years later. Athens was now the first state in Greece and developed against Persia a defensive confederacy which she grew in time to look upon as an empire; her allies were regarded rather as subjects. The latter part of the century was to see a prolonged clash—the Peloponnesian War (431–404 B.C.)—between a democratic Athens which had waxed imperial and proud and the authoritarian régime of Sparta which resented Athenian pretensions.

The sixty years after the battle of Marathon were a period of great cultural enlightenment and beauty at Athens, for which one man in particular was responsible—Pericles. He spent vast sums on statues of the gods and on temples; such gratitude was right, he argued, in return for deliverance from the Persian menace. The richer citizens undertook various offices on behalf of the community; each wealthy burgher in turn, for example, had to fit out a galley for the fleet and train the rowers. The wealthy also paid for the official deputations sent from time to time to Delphi or the temple of Apollo at Delos, or to the great Pan-Hellenic festivals. At their cost the choruses which performed at the annual dramatic festivals held at Athens in honour of the god Dionysus were trained and equipped. Among the most distinguished authors contributing to Attic drama at this time were Aeschylus, Sophocles and Euripides (tragedians), and Aristophanes (comic poet). The Periclean age at Athens achieved an astonishingly high level of civilisation; architecture, sculpture and literature flourished, and Athenians were proud to identify themselves with their successful city.

With increased prosperity the Athenians now enjoyed more

leisure. They were fond of argument and discussion, and the large questions concerning right and wrong, truth, man in society, etc., came to be canvassed with great energy and seriousness. The Sophists (a convenient label—*sophist* by this time meant essentially someone professing specialised knowledge—but we must not think of them as a unified body) paid much attention to the qualities required in a citizen. Under democracy every free citizen had a right to express his views in the assembly, but clearly the power of effective speech was not something equally possessed by all as a natural endowment. Many Sophists set up as instructors in public speaking, a pursuit in which they came under heavy attack from some quarters for teaching their pupils to make mere debating points without regard to the truth. The charge was not groundless. Even so, the investigation of the ways to rhetorical efficiency was far from being a sterile exercise, for it had wider effects; various other departments of knowledge were opened up and explored (logic, grammar, linguistic theory, etc.); and furthermore, important cultural, political and ethical issues were raised and brought to notice by the work of the Sophists in general. They took their stance upon a broad, humanistic platform.

Specially noteworthy amongst the issues was whether the dictates of morality proceeded from nature (*physis*) or from mutable convention (*nomos*). Is moral duty related to an unwritten natural law, divine and eternal? Is social justice an artificial compact to protect the weak against the strong? Is might by nature right? The discussions initiated on such themes by Sophists were to continue reverberating, as we shall see from some of the extracts given later.

In the dramatists, primary issues in man's moral life were treated from differing viewpoints. Aeschylus (525–456 B.C.) reflected much on divine authority and the concept of justice. Sophocles (*c.* 496–406 B.C.) considered the problem of suffering in relation to great and noble spirits, while the intellectually restless and didactic Euripides (*c.* 485–406 B.C.) studied human nature with a special eye for its morbidities. In comedy Aristophanes (*c.* 445–385 B.C.) with brilliant and uproarious satire flayed demagogues, war-mongers, self-seekers and other kinds of people he found malignant in contemporary Athens.

The intellectual scepticism of the Sophists made a deep impression on Euripides, but Aristophanes shared the view that the Sophistic movement had had an unhealthy influence.

Herodotus, who came to Athens in 446 B.C. after many travels, treated in his pioneering historical work the powerful struggle between East and West, barbarian and Greek, which culminated in the Persian War. Thucydides, himself an Athenian citizen, wrote a dispassionate history of the Peloponnesian War down to 411 B.C., giving not only an accurate and concise account of the events but also a clear statement of their causes, with the political and moral lessons they convey. Between these two historians came the decline of Athens and the age of intellectual revolution begun by the sophists. There is in Herodotus' work, as it traces the humbling of Persian pride, an expansive, romantic element; Thucydides' austere, analytical study with its penetrating observations on Greek political life carries quite a different atmosphere. The Peloponnesian War marks a decisive turning-point in the story of the Greek *polis;* the fourth century was to witness great changes in the way of thinking and living among the Greeks.

A commanding figure in Greek thought, Socrates (470–399 B.C.) wrote nothing, but had widespread and lasting influence. Plato was deeply indebted to him. Stressing the moral responsibility of the individual, he stimulated the Athenians with his gently persistent and ironical questioning to think about the conduct of life and to question accepted values. Charged in 399 B.C. with impiety and corrupting the youth, he faced the death sentence with perfect courage holding that as the state had reared him it had the right to judge him.

Plato (427–347 B.C.), founder of a school under the name of the Academy, expounded his system in his *Dialogues*, the most famous of which is the *Republic*, a sketch of his ideal state. Plato's studies of the state are chiefly concerned with the character and education of its rulers. In the well-ordered soul, he argues, the three parts are ranged in a certain succession: wisdom and the love of it predominate, while passion and the desire for glory and victory are subordinate to reason but yet superior to appetite. Happiness and self-fulfilment depend upon this inner order, and by analogy in the good society there ought to be three functional classes: law-givers or guardians, protectors, producers. In Plato's constitution national power and wealth will be administered for the benefit of the whole community. This ideal he puts forward as a standard for evaluating already existing societies. The concentration of authority in the hands of an expert body of legislators has often attracted adverse criticism as being totalitarian, but in *Republic* IV Plato expressly recognises the principle of popular consent. Plato is not so anti-individual as has been alleged, though he does look upon the individual without the body politic as a mere fragment of no special significance.

For Aristotle (384–322 B.C.), originally a pupil of Plato, man realises his full potentiality as a human being when he participates in a community. In his biological investigations Aristotle had observed the phenomenon of growth reaching completion in some clear end or purpose; applying the same thinking to politics, he concluded that the proper end for the state was that condition in which the citizen could attain the good life and enjoy happiness. The family, the local community and the state are the setting in which the citizen is enabled to fulfil himself properly. What on a small scale is the good of the individual becomes on a larger scale the good of the citizen and of society at large. The citizen of the best state is the man who has the power and the resolve to govern and be governed for the sake of the life in accordance with virtue (see p. 34 ff.).

The tendency of Platonism was to ascribe priority to ideas and pure thought, but Aristotle gave his attention to the world of things and experience.

For both Plato and Aristotle the Greek city-state represented the most natural and therefore the ideal community. Aristotle would have been dismayed at the huge communities which came into existence in the empire of his pupil, Alexander the Great. For Plato the ideal state numbered 5,000 citizens; Aristotle's was one in which the citizens would be able to know each other by sight. Greek city-states were small. Only three had a total of more than 20,000 citizens—Syracuse and Acragas (the modern Girgenti) in Sicily, and Athens itself, which, including the surrounding region of Attica, is estimated to have had 315,000 inhabitants at the start of the Peloponnesian War. Of these half, consisting of men, women and children, were Athenian, approximately a tenth resident aliens, and the rest slaves.

As a political thinker Aristotle differs greatly on some points from his master. Plato thinks largely in terms of the whole community's happiness, whereas Aristotle puts his emphasis on the needs of the individual; for him the state exists for the individual's benefit. The communal possession of wives, children and goods, which Plato advocates for the ruling class, he rejects, seeing the importance for human beings of personal associations, ties and ownership.

Plato's chief insistence is on knowledge (as opposed to the unexamined assumptions of traditional opinion), and he attempts to place it on a solid basis of logic. Civic virtue is a matter of study and knowledge to be pursued by a specialist class who will be able to impart their knowledge. Plato's system thus calls for intense specialisation and division of function. Aristotle, while recognising the need for these in political life and accepting that natural gifts and acquired capacities are necessary for the business of politics, yet feels that Plato's claims for moral and political virtue as branches of knowledge on the same footing as medicine and navigation are exaggerated.

The Greek was an individualist, in strong contradistinction to the Roman who generally was conformist in his attitude. But the Greek's individualism was exercised within the framework of a group whether that of the city-state or of kinship, cult or locality; he liked both to have a share in what was happening and to engage in rivalry. The fourth century witnessed a distinct growth in Greek individualism. Sculpture starts to be more introspective, ceasing to try to represent the universal and turning to the particular. Drama shows the same tendency with its increased interest in studying men and not Man. In philosophy the central question has become 'How ought we to live?' Cynics, Cyrenaics, Stoics and Epicureans joined in the search for an answer. The Stoics taught the interdependence of mankind and as a consequence participation in politics as a prime duty for the wise man. But the *polis* was figuring less and less in serious thought; the concept of the *cosmopolis* or world-city, which the conquests of Alexander the Great (d. 323 B.C.) did much to encourage, now came into play, and the Stoic idea of a 'city of Zeus' and of the brotherhood of mankind (their most important contribution to practical morality) gained influence. In Old Comedy the life of the *polis* had been exposed mercilessly to the sharpest criticism through the medium of satire and burlesque, but in New Comedy the themes relate to private and domestic situations. The individual citizen is by now preoccupied with his own needs and concerns.

In the matter of religion, we may note briefly in conclusion, the deep strain of individualism in the Greek mentality and the accompanying sense of the group find particular expression. The mystery religions (secret cults involving initiation and mystic ideas about the life-giving powers of nature) spoke to the condition of the individual, while the Olympian religion with its multiplicity of divinities who though invisible were yet considered members of the community appealed to the group.

THE ROMAN SITUATION

The author Livy (59 B.C.–A.D. 17) in the Preface to his work on Roman history remarks that no nation more repays study than Rome, for in no other did uprightness of character and primitive simplicity so long resist the corruptions of luxury and wealth. This is a common theme amongst Roman writers. After the long struggle against Carthage which ended in 146 B.C. Rome was the strongest power in the world as then known to Romans, having completed her conquest of the East, Greece, Africa and Spain. The chief cause of this rise to greatness was undoubtedly the citizens' real devotion to the state. Every citizen saw it as his first duty to serve the Republic; Roman generals, true to this spirit, had sought for distinction not so much for themselves as for Rome. But empire brought trade and wealth, and wealth brought selfishness. The public spirit characteristic of older times was forgotten as men scrambled to make fortunes. The gap between the rich and the poor steadily grew wider, and Rome was crowded with people from throughout Italy hoping to make money there, or at least to find employment. With the vast increase in the slave traffic from the various conquered lands work for the Italian and Roman poor was becoming scarcer. Slaves (or freed slaves) performed a great many skilled or semi-skilled jobs, and were employed on the farms and in the mines. From being a land of peasants and small farmers Italy had greatly changed. Successive wars had called away the smallholders and ploughmen; the land lay uncultivated—or it had been seized by magnates who by means of huge gangs of slaves worked the large estates they thus formed. Farmers returning from military service often were unable to find work even as ordinary labourers. Most of the common land had been taken over by the rich.

In view of this situation, the brothers Tiberius and Gaius Gracchus, from one of the oldest and noblest Roman families, attempted a programme of reform. Tiberius, as one of the tribunes or representatives of the people, proposed an agrarian law designed to check the nobles' avarice and use of slave labour. The public land was to be redistributed on an equitable basis at low rents amongst the needy, and the fortune of Attalus, king of Pergamus, unexpectedly bequeathed in this year (133 B.C.) to the Roman people, was to be used for equipping the farms. But though his bill was passed and a commission appointed to carry out its terms, a riot was set on foot by his aristocratic opponents when Tiberius tried to secure re-election as tribune and he was killed.

Gaius as tribune in 123 and 122 B.C. took up the cause. He at once renewed his brother's agrarian law, began a colonisation scheme, and distributed cheap corn. Amongst other legislation he enacted that the *iudices* or jurymen should be drawn from the knights (*equites*) or middle class, and not as before from the Senate (the supreme council of state). Resistance was bitter and strong; Gaius failed to win re-election for 121 B.C.; his acts were impeached by his enemies, and he was killed in an ensuing riot in the Forum (122 B.C.). So began a century of strife which was to see the downfall of the Roman republic itself.

Strife was of course no new thing in Roman history, but the

Romans had somehow been able to direct and control it, so that it did not leave the state defenceless before external aggression or unable to prevent internal disintegration. After the abolition of the monarchy at Rome (traditionally in 509 B.C.) a republican system of government was established which was to endure for 500 years. The first half of this period was marked by bitter conflict between the Roman nobility (patricians) and commons (plebeians). The plebeians at first spent sixty years in defeating the harsh and systematic exploitation to which they were subjected, and the next century and a half in struggling to secure political and economic equality with the patricians. Full social equality was always to elude them; the patrician families liked to remain aloof.

By the time of the Gracchi it was the Roman Senate, which has been likened to the House of Lords, that ruled Rome. The popular assemblies (*comitia*) were by nature too unwieldy to make proper discussion possible, and the mass of citizens ignorant or ill-informed about the many matters on which they were expected to have an opinion and vote. In the Senate alone was real decision-making on the governing of state and empire possible.

Powerful individuals, driven by ruthless and selfish ambition, now challenged successively the authority of the state. Marius (157–86 B.C.) was tribune of the people in 119 B.C. and became one of the chief popular leaders at Rome. Elected consul, or principal officer of state (and the constitution laid down that there should be two consuls at a time), in 107 B.C., he conducted a successful campaign in North Africa against the Numidian king Jugurtha. Marius inaugurated the rise of a professional class of soldier whose interest it was to stir up and prolong wars. He clashed with Sulla (138–78 B.C.), who was originally on his military staff, in the first great Civil War at Rome (88–82 B.C.). Since the death of the Gracchi, Senate and political leaders working through the people had been engaged in strife; the Senate were trying to preserve things as they were, the others were seeking more power. Many of the leaders, however, on either side had little regard for the good of the state, intent upon furthering their own schemes. Marius had taken the popular side because he had been rebuffed by the patricians in the

Senate. Sulla stood for the Senate, and when Rome and the whole of Italy were in his hands he made his first objectives the restoration of public order and the return to the Senate of its former power, a process in which nearly 5,000 people were proscribed and killed.

The old aristocrats had largely disappeared under the onslaught and proscriptions of Marius, and of the prominent men now in Rome most were young with no special reverence for the old order of things. A leading exception was Marcus Tullius Cicero (106–43 B.C.), the great orator, who vigorously upheld the cause of the Senate, though being of humble origin he never succeeded in winning its full trust. As a politician Cicero failed, for he was not naturally a leader and he consistently found it difficult to reach decisions and hold fast by them.

Selfish individualism, working to the pattern set by Marius and Sulla in their deadly rivalry and striving for mastery of the state and its resources, now becomes the main feature of events. Great captains with huge armies behind them fight it out for the prize. In 60 B.C. the three most powerful men of the time, Julius Caesar, Pompey the Great and Marcus Crassus, formed an arrangement to advance their private ends. They coolly made dispositions affecting the whole state as though they had every right to do so, and they renewed their arrangements in 56 B.C. But it was already growing very clear that the Roman world was not big enough to hold both Caesar and Pompey at once. Open war broke out and Pompey suffered final defeat at the battle of Pharsalus in northern Greece (48 B.C.). Caesar now commanded the whole scene, but in 44 B.C. he fell under the assassins' daggers, strongly suspected of regal ambition. One of the most generally able and remarkable men of antiquity, Caesar, during the time of absolute power which he wielded from 48 B.C. till his death, as officially designated *dictator* (ruler armed with unlimited authority to deal with an emergency) worked very hard to resolve the many problems facing the state. He improved the laws and reformed the army, the navy, the treasury and the law courts. His rule was mild, beneficent, just. But his rise to eminence had been at the expense of the community.

The next stage in the civil conflict is dominated by Caesar's great-nephew and heir Octavian who waged war against the republican assassins. A dozen years of varied campaigns were to pass until in 31 B.C. at the battle of Actium Octavian emerged as complete victor over his enemies and undisputed master of the Roman world. The Republic was now dead. In 27 B.C. Octavian assumed the title of emperor, 'Augustus' being henceforth his official designation.

The causes which led to general acquiescence in the change from Republic to Empire are not hard to understand. The universal weariness and insecurity made people desire peace at any price; the long years of civil war had been a dreadful burden, and one contender for power seemed to ordinary people much the same as another. People too had become used to rule by one man, but Augustus was shrewd enough to keep the outward form of the Republic while taking all real power into his own hands. Men were happy to close their eyes to the thinly veiled absolutism, grateful that one man had been able to crush his rivals decisively and pacify the world. Further, the traditional methods of government (through the Senate and the popular assemblies) had proved unequal to the task of administering a world empire; the need for one strong organising will above the jealousies and quarrels of individuals was clamant. And the vastness of the empire itself demanded centralised control; provincial misgovernment was rife, rapacious officials plundering at will the areas assigned to them.

Julius Caesar had devised in most of its details the scheme which Augustus put into operation, but he was not tactful (or guileful) enough. Augustus was more astute, representing what was in fact despotism as a continuance of the former ways. The Augustan régime showed great skill in its use of propaganda, and it was able to attract men of literary genius (Virgil, Horace, Livy) to publicise its ideals. For ideals it did have, despite its dubious credentials. Augustus saw that a return to the plain living and high thinking of earlier days was utterly necessary; the nation's morale had to be restored, and the ancient virtues of frugality, good faith and industry cultivated afresh. In his *Odes* (especially 1–6 of the third book) Horace emphasises these moral themes, calling on the citizens to revive the old values in the community.

In his great epic poem, the *Aeneid* (named after Aeneas, its chief figure), Virgil treats the legend of Rome's founding with much symbolism and many glances at the contemporary situation. In Aeneas, who has great dangers and difficulties to face in the performance of his immense task, the poet gives us the portrait of a vocation; Aeneas is a man who learns that the way of virtue is sacrifice and that he must subordinate his own happiness and comfort to the common good. Livy's *History* invites comparison as the prose counterpart of the *Aeneid*. It is a celebration of the achievement of the Roman people, designed to excite enthusiasm in Roman minds for the glorious past and all that it meant.

Augustus died in A.D. 14. Under his successors during the first century many of the worst faults of monarchical absolutism became evident. Personal freedom was more and more circumscribed, the community increasingly subjected to the will (or whimsy) of one man. During this time the religious philosophy of Stoicism began to have wider and deeper effect amongst thinking men at Rome. A pantheistic system, teaching that the whole universe was permeated by a divine, vital and rational principle in the form of hot breath or air in which all men shared alike, its centre of gravity was its ethics. Since all men participate in the divine reason they are all therefore brothers, and so Stoicism preached a liberal humanitarianism embracing both bond and free and the necessity for the citizen to take a share in political life. Virtue for them meant living in accordance with the divine plan as witnessed in and by the natural order, and moral proficiency was independent of one's external circumstances. Slavery they condemned as unnatural, but they did not seek to abolish it. It was spiritual freedom in which they were really interested.

The social philosophy of Stoicism stressed the importance of the individual and thus stood in sharp contrast to the arbitrary and irresponsible rule of the principate which rode roughshod over personal rights. There was a strong Stoic opposition. Under Stoic influence a new spirit of philanthropy, though far from being universal, was abroad. Lucius Annaeus Seneca the

younger (*c.* 5 B.C.–A.D. 65) was engaged in high politics, being
in succession the emperor Nero's tutor and chief minister ; and
no doubt the spread of Stoic ideas in this age was to some
extent due to the devoted zeal of this eminent man who wrote
numerous works expounding his school's principles.

This same century saw the rise of Christianity which became
in the fourth century the official religion of the Roman Empire
and in which the problem of the individual and the community
is firmly grasped: the unique value of the individual is
asserted, while his responsibility to the wider community is
clearly stated. The rights of a person as a person and the claims
of society have to be held in balance. Christianity brought
spiritual democracy into the world by insisting on love as the
highest virtue—costly love, that is, which is quite different from
mere sentimentality but which actively seeks the other person's
good. There is a certain resemblance between Stoic and Christian ethics, but the theologies are far apart.

The Christian thinker Augustine spent the years A.D. 413–
426 over the twenty-two books of *The City of God*, a review of
history from the Christian position which was to provide the
Middle Ages with a political theory and an ideal. Its occasion
was the capture and sack of Rome by the barbarians (A.D. 410),
and its aim was to rebut the pagan charge that Christianity had
weakened Roman power to resist. Augustine devotes ten books
to showing how the traditional gods of the Romans have failed
to protect them or contribute to their moral well-being, and in
the remaining twelve he discusses the two cities: Jerusalem, the
City of God, which is the Christian Church, and Babylon, the
earthly (and pagan) state. Limitations of time or country do not
restrict the progress of the eternal City whose citizenship is
intended for all men equally and in which all are equally
esteemed. Its consummation will be achieved only at the end
of time when Christ shall gather his elect into his kingdom.
Augustine's conception is of a universal society whose members
are tied to one another by the bonds of Christian love.

In summing up the Roman outlook and civilisation, the main
feature that strikes the observer is their respect for constituted

authority of any kind. Romans were imbued with a profound sense of community and the need for conformity and self-discipline in the members. Throughout the early stages of their history personal and sectional interests were subordinated to the good of the country. A key word in understanding the Romans is *gravitas*, which refers to the bearing of a man of worth and authority who respects himself and the authority possessed by others, and claims in turn their respect. The word *virtus* (virtue) was not, as the Greeks understood virtue, supreme excellence in the art of living, but manly courage chiefly in war, but also in the political arena. The word *pietas* is peculiarly Roman in its application: meaning firstly dutiful respect and affection for a father, it came to include the dutiful regard a member of a family ought to feel towards the others, both living and dead. Respect for tradition, whether in the family or in the state, was characteristic of the Romans, and the linking together of the generations by the sense of 'piety' gave stability to society. *Pietas* meant, too, dutiful worship of the gods and loyalty to their will. Every sense of *pietas* is exemplified by Aeneas in Virgil's great nationalistic epic, the *Aeneid*.

In the second century B.C. the sudden wealth arising from the new conquests upset the moral equilibrium of many at Rome. Similarly, in our own age and society a sudden win on the football pools has often given rise to numerous problems for the unprepared punter. And yet, despite the rivalries and ambitions of self-seeking individuals, the Romans did not entirely forget their own corporate ideals and primitive virtues. Whatever excesses were committed, there were always some who cherished and kept alive the old national conceptions about honour and justice, loyalty and endurance.

RETROSPECT

In Greek civilisation the individual gradually emerges through various political stages. It is not possible to generalise from any one city-state, for they all differed considerably amongst themselves; but to regard Athens as the finest instance of the type is wholly justifiable. Popular rule through the Assembly which was open to all free citizens was a reality during the fifth and fourth centuries B.C. But the seeds of corruption were already present; democracy became flaccid. And then the vast power of Alexander's empire and the Hellenistic kingships grew up to deprive the *polis* generally of its status and function of leadership in Greek politics. Monarchical authority had returned again.

Rome's history shows a movement from exclusive patricianism to a qualified democracy, followed by a long period of intensely ambitious individualism excited by the prospect of power and wealth. At last, the wearied nation was glad to settle for a disguised absolutism which in time grew openly despotic.

Part Two

I The Framework of Society

In the third book of his great work, chapter 61, Herodotus reaches the reign of Darius, king of Persia 521–485 B.C., who was defeated by the Greeks at Marathon. To make matters clear he gives an account of preceding events, the death of king Cambyses (Darius' predecessor) and the overthrow by Darius of the usurper, Gaumata the Magian (member of the Persian priestly clan), who was impersonating Smerdis, the dead brother of Cambyses. In chapters 80 to 83 the conspirators are made to debate what kind of constitution should be adopted. The discussion is set in sixth-century Persia, but it refers to political science as practised by fifth-century Greeks. The question of the constitution was central for Greek political thought, and the discussion in Herodotus is the earliest extant one on the theme. It is not improbable that such a debate took place, but the account in Herodotus is fictionalised, composed after the manner of fifth-century Greek philosophers. When Otanes urges the merits of democracy he is actually referring to *Athenian* democracy, and when monarchy is discussed the reference is in fact to *tyranny* amongst the Greeks (see p. 6f.). The claims of democracy, oligarchy and monarchy are advanced; monarchy wins, and Darius after a skilful manœuvre becomes sole ruler. Here is the whole dialogue:

When the tumult had subsided and five days had elapsed, those who had risen up against the Magi deliberated on the state of affairs, and speeches were delivered which are disbelieved by some of the Greeks but were made all the same. Otanes recommended that they should commit the government to the Persians at large, speaking as follows: 'I think that no one amongst us should hereafter be a monarch since monarchy is neither agreeable nor good. For you know to what a pitch the insolence of Cambyses grew, and you have experienced the insolence of the Magus. How can a monarchy

be an ethically well-founded government when it allows a man
to do whatever he likes without any control or responsibility?
Even the best of men invested with such power would change
for the worse and not see things as he used to. For insolence is
engendered in him by the advantages which surround him,
and envy is implanted in him from his birth, and having these
two he has every vice. Puffed up with insolence he commits
many presumptuous acts, and others through envy. And yet
we should have expected that a man holding absolute authority
would be free from envy since he has every advantage. But the
opposite occurs in his attitude towards the citizens, for he feels
a grudge against the best merely for continuing to live and
takes pleasure in the worst men of the nation. He is very ready
to listen to tale-bearers, and is the most inconsistent of all men.
If you show him respect in moderation he is offended because
he is not receiving enough honour; and if anyone honours him
very much he takes offence because he thinks he is being
flattered. But the worst of all is this—he changes ancestral
tradition, violates women, and executes men without trial. But
government by the people has as its mark that very lovely
word, equality; and secondly it is guilty of none of the excesses
that a monarch is. The magistrate is appointed by lot and is
held responsible for his conduct in office, and refers all plans to
the people. For these reasons I propose that we abolish the
monarchy and raise the people to power, for all things reside
in the many.' This was the view that Otanes put forward, but
Megabyzus advised them to entrust the government to an
oligarchy in this speech: 'I agree with what Otanes has said
about abolishing the monarchy [literally, 'tyranny']; but in
urging us to transfer power to the people he is mistaken.
Nothing is more foolish and ignorant than a useless crowd. It is
utterly unendurable that men who are trying to escape the
insolence of a tyrant should fall under the insolence of an
unrestrained multitude. A tyrant does at least act consciously
and of set purpose, but the mob does not have the means of
knowing. How should it when it has neither been taught nor
has any idea of what is right and proper? Rushing on blindly
without reflection it precipitates affairs like a winter torrent. Let those, then, who are ill-disposed to the Persians

adopt a democracy; but let us, having chosen an association of the best men, hand over power to them, for we shall ourselves be included in their number, and it is reasonable to expect that the best advice will come from the best men.'

Darius was the third to speak. 'I agree,' he said, 'with everything that Megabyzus has said concerning the masses, but I do not accept his opinion about oligarchy. Consider the three forms of government before us—democracy, oligarchy, monarchy—and suppose each to be the best of its kind; I maintain that the last is far superior. For nothing can be found better than one man, provided that he is the best for the job. Possessed of a judgment in keeping with his character he would govern the people without blame, and he would keep measures against traitors secret more easily than any other kind of government. In an oligarchy where many men are in competition with one another to gain distinction in the public service strong personal feuds are the usual result; each one wishes to be chief and to see his own proposals carried, and thus they form deep animosities against one another, from which seditions arise; and from seditions bloodshed. And from that state of affairs the only way out is to return to rule by one man—a clear sign that monarchy is best. But when the people rule malpractices inevitably occur; in this case, however, corruption in public service results not in private antipathies but in firm personal alliances, for the men responsible for it act in concert; and this lasts until someone or other of the people comes forward and puts them down; and on this account he is admired by the people, and being admired he is soon acknowledged as a ruler with absolute power—which too shows that monarchy is best. To sum up my argument: where did our freedom come from, and who gave us it? Is it the result of democracy or oligarchy or rule by one man? It was one man who set us free, and in my opinion that is the form of government we should preserve—that is, without changing ancient laws which have proved their worth. That would be a disastrous course.'

These were the three views set out in the speeches, and the four men who had not spoken voted for the last. Otanes, who had supported equality before the law (*isonomia*), made another speech when the decision went against him. 'Colleagues,' he said, 'it is clear that one of us will be the king (*basileus*), either appointed by lot, or by the people of Persia exercising its choice amongst us, or by some other method. I shall not enter into competition with you for the crown, for I wish neither to govern nor to be governed. But I waive all claim to the government of the nation on this condition, that neither I nor any of my descendants shall be made subject to that one of you, whoever it is, who is made king.'

(Herodotus, 3. 80–3)

By the fifth century B.C. the majority of city-states had attained a more or less democratic constitution; the idea of freedom, law and equality had taken root—the word *isonomia* was in fact sometimes used to signify democracy (as above in this passage which, we must remember, while ostensibly referring to sixth-century Persia, really deals with fifth-century Greece). What kind of democracy? Not one in which all adults participated in the government, but one in which all adult, free male *citizens* had the right to participate; the usual Greek qualification for citizenship was that one's father (if not mother also) should have been a citizen, for in theory and in sentiment the 'state' for a Greek was a body of kinsmen.

The modern conception of democracy involves universal adult suffrage, but because of the size of the population we have to delegate government to a few representatives, which is a form of oligarchy.

A further point: while *demokratia* meant 'rule by the people', in the political theorists, especially Plato and Aristotle, it acquired the significance 'rule by the poor' and was thus seen as a bad thing—a kind of inverted oligarchy or tyranny implying government in accordance with self-interest.

THE GOOD OLD DAYS

Isocrates, the pamphleteer and highly influential Athenian teacher of rhetoric (436–338 B.C.), considered that Athens had been at its best in the good old days of Solon (see p. 10) under the wholesome influence of the ancient Court of the Areopagus (the oldest Council at Athens, originating in the king's advisory body of leading men). This sentimental regard for the past—and not a few shared it—arose from disgust at the excesses of democratic individualism in fourth-century Athens (see p. 15 f.). In his essay called *Areopagiticus* Isocrates presents an idealised 'ancestral constitution' with criticism of the existing political situation. He believes that 'freedom' has gone too far—hence the city's troubles. He condemns pure democracy and advocates a return to the restricted democracy under Solon and under Cleisthenes in the sixth century, when the people had sovereign authority to choose its leaders but only from those citizens who were qualified. These leaders were strictly answerable for their actions in office.

For Isocrates' élitist tone we may compare Pericles' Funeral Oration (see p. 56 f.). As was typical in ancient Greece as a whole, democracy in Athens was a highly exclusive form of government even at its most developed stage. Isocrates longs for the powers of censorship once wielded by the Court of the Areopagus over public and private morals to be restored in order to check the anarchic tendencies in contemporary Athenian society which seemed attributable to excessive popular liberty. To some extent the same problem—how to balance private rights and public needs—confronts democracy in many parts of the modern world. How far should libertarianism go? Are we in danger of turning the democratic ideal into an idol? Can we have too much 'democracy'?

The extracts given cover the main points in Isocrates' discussion:

We all know that prosperity does not come to and remain with those who have surrounded themselves with the finest and strongest walls, nor with those who have collected the greatest population into one place, but rather with those who govern their city most nobly and intelligently. For the soul of a city is nothing other than its constitution, having as much power over it as does the mind over the body. For it is this which deliberates over all matters, attempting to preserve the good features and keeping clear of what is disastrous. It is to this of necessity that the laws, the public orators and the private citizens are assimilated, and all the members of the community prosper or fare ill in accordance with the kind of constitution under which they live. . . .

Our ancestors had decided that the people as the overlord of the state should appoint the magistrates, punish those in default and judge in cases of dispute; while those citizens who could afford the time and had sufficient means should look after the affairs of the community as servants of the people, deserving praise if they loyally carried out their commission, and being content with this honour, but on the other hand finding no mercy if they governed badly, but receiving the severest punishment. And how could one find a democracy more stable or more just than this, which appointed the most able men to look after its affairs, but gave the people power over their rulers? . . .

What contributed most to the good government of the state for our ancestors was that of the two acknowledged kinds of equality (the one which gives the same to all alike, and the one which gives to each man what is appropriate to him) they recognised which was the more useful; and rejecting as unjust that which considers the good and bad as worthy of the same awards, they preferred that which rewards or punishes each man according to his merits. They governed the city on this system, not making appointments by lot to the various offices from amongst all the citizens (as became the practice later), but choosing the best and most able for each particular function. For they expected that the rest of the citizens would take on the character of those put in charge of affairs. Further, they thought that this method of making appointments was also more democratic than the method that depended on the casting of lots, because with the system of election by lot fortune would decide the issue and those who were eager for oligarchy would often obtain the offices. But under the scheme of selecting the worthiest men the people would have the power to choose those who were most devoted to the existing constitution.

The reason why this plan was acceptable to the majority and why the offices did not become a source of quarrelling was that they had been trained to work hard and to be economical, and not to neglect their own possessions and plot to seize the property of others, and not to look to public funds for the balancing of their domestic budgets,[1] but rather to assist the

---

[1] A reference to the payment not only of magistrates but of those who attended the Assembly or served as jurymen. Aristotle (*Constitution of Athens* 24) says that after the reforms of Aristides (478 B.C.) over 20,000 Athenians made their living as state employees in one way or another.

commonwealth should the need arise from their own private resources, and not to know more accurately the incomes derived from public offices than those which accrued to them from their own private holdings. So rigorously did they keep their hands off what belonged to the state that it was harder in those times to find men who were willing to hold office than it is now to find men who are not seeking the privilege. For they did not consider the charge over public affairs as an opportunity to enrich themselves but as a service to the state; nor did they try to discover from their first day in office whether their predecessors had by oversight omitted any source of profit but much rather whether they had neglected any piece of urgent state business. . . .

The poorer amongst the citizens were so far from envying the more affluent that they were as much concerned for the great estates as for their own, thinking that the prosperity of the rich was the key to their own well-being. The possessors of wealth did not look contemptuously upon those in a less favourable position, but treating poverty amongst their fellow-citizens as a reproach to themselves, they would assist the needy, handing over lands to some at moderate rents, sending out some to engage in trade, and giving others the means to take up various occupations. For they had no fear that they might suffer one of two things—that they might lose all their investments or recover only after much trouble a mere fraction of what they had paid out. . . . The result of their dealing fairly with one another was that the possession of property was secured to those to whom it legally belonged, but its usufruct was available in common to all those in need amongst the body of citizens. . . .

But in fact, they believed, virtue is not increased by written laws but by the habits of day-to-day living. For most people assimilate the customs and morals amongst which they have been brought up. In addition, they reckoned that multitudes of laws defined in minute terms are a sign that the state is being badly administered; for it is in the endeavour to construct barriers against the spread of crime that men in this kind of state are impelled to introduce many laws. But those who are correctly governed do not require to fill their colonnades with

written statutes but simply to cherish justice in their souls. For
it is not by legislation but by sound morals that cities are well
governed, since those who have been badly reared will venture
to break even those laws which have been drawn up with close
attention to detail, while those who have been well brought up
will be willing to abide by even a simple set of rules.

(Isocrates, *Areopagiticus* 13–41 excerpted)

Other items in Isocrates' scheme are that education of the young is a
primary duty of the state, but since only the affluent will hold office,
only they need a higher education; and that the state should take its
religious duties seriously. His views are highly conservative, and his
programme was hardly feasible in the Athens of his time, his assess-
ment of the earlier age being too comfortably optimistic and so out of
focus. He sees sixth-century Athens bathed in a roseate hue.

We turn now to the *Politics* of Aristotle. The first book combats
Plato's communism (see p. 80 ff.). The state, says Aristotle, is not
merely a large family, nor does it owe its existence merely to convention (an answer to sophistic doctrine, see p. 12; and compare the
'Melian Debate', p. 59 ff.): he affirms that man is *by nature* a social
being, and this emphasis on the natural is found throughout (e.g. in
the discussion on slavery, p. 39 ff.). The second book offers criticism of
certain of Plato's views in the *Republic* and the *Laws*. The third book,
in a Platonic, or rather Socratic, spirit considers such questions as
'What is the state?', 'What is a citizen?', 'Is the good man the same as
the good citizen?', and then goes on to give a classification of forms
of government based on the one in Plato's *Politicus*. The fourth, fifth
and sixth books, possibly under the influence of Aristotle's biological
researches, consider practical details in existing constitutions, and the
great amount of constitutional detail contained in the middle books
no doubt reflects that survey. In the seventh and eighth books Aristotle passes on to the ideal state, enquiring into the matter under
various headings (external conditions, population size, classes,
education).

Virtue or excellence (*areté*), a key conception, is for Aristotle 'a state
of character concerned with choice, lying in a mean relative to ourselves (i.e., the famous 'Golden Mean'), determined by a rational
principle and in the way in which the man of practical wisdom would
determine it.' *Areté* is thus rooted in habit. The state exists for the sake

of the good life or, an equivalent term, self-sufficiency (*autarkeia*) which Aristotle defines thus: 'By self-sufficient we do not mean that which is sufficient for a single person leading a solitary life. We include parents, children, wife, and friends and fellow-citizens at large, since man is born for citizenship.' All men, he says, naturally seek happiness which is itself 'an activity in accordance with *areté*'. Man's greatest opportunity for achieving happiness lies in the state or *polis*; ethics and politics formed one subject for Aristotle.

In studying the following extracts from Aristotle's *Politics* the reader should consider how far the disappearance of the ancient city-state makes the work one of purely historical interest. The reader should also compare Aristotle's ideas about the purpose of the state with those current today.

THE STATE AND OTHER COMMUNITIES: THE DIFFERENCE

Every state is, as we see, a kind of partnership, and every partnership is established with a view to some good; for mankind always acts in order to obtain that which they think good. But if all partnerships aim at some good, the state or political association, which is the highest of all and which includes all the others, aims at good in a greater degree than any other, and at the highest good.

Some people believe that the qualifications of a statesman, king, householder, and master are the same, and that they differ, not in kind, but only in the number of their subjects— that is, that the ruler over a few people is called a master, over more the manager of a household, over more still a statesman or king, as if there were no difference between a large household and a small state. The following is the distinction which is made between the statesman and the king: when the government is personal the ruler is a king; when, according to the rules of the science of politics, the citizens rule and are ruled in turn, then he is called a statesman.

But all this is a mistaken view; that governments differ in kind will be evident if we examine the matter in accordance with our regular method of investigation. As in every other department of science, so in politics, it is necessary to resolve the composite whole down to its uncompounded elements or least parts of the whole. We must therefore look at the elements composing the state the better to discern in what the different kinds of rule differ from one another, and whether any scientific result can be obtained about each one of them.

Here, as elsewhere, the best system of examination will be to begin at the beginning and observe things in their growth.

In the first place there must be a union of those who cannot exist without one another, namely, of male and female so that the species may continue (and this is a union that takes place not of deliberate purpose, but because with man as with the other animals and with plants there is a natural instinct to desire to leave behind one an image of oneself), and of natural ruler and subject for the sake of security. For that which can foresee by the exercise of mind is by nature intended to be ruler and master, while that which can with its body give effect to such foresight is a subject and naturally a slave; hence master and slave have the same interest. Nature has distinguished between the female and the slave, for nature is not niggardly, like the cutler who shapes the Delphian knife for many purposes; she makes each thing for a single use, and every instrument is best made when it is intended for one and not for many uses. Yet among barbarians the female and the slave are on the same footing because barbarians have no class of natural rulers, but they are a community of slaves, male and female. Hence the saying of the poet:

'It is fitting that Greeks should rule over barbarians',
implying that barbarian and slave are the same in nature.

Out of these two partnerships between man and woman, master and slave, the first thing to arise is the family or household, and Hesiod is right when he says:

'First and foremost a house and a wife and an ox for the plough',
for the ox is the poor man's slave. The family is the association provided by nature to meet men's everyday needs, and the members of it are called by Charondas 'companions of the meal-tub' and by the Cretan Epimenides 'companions of the manger'. But when several families are united and the association aims at something more than the supply of daily needs,

the first society to come into existence is the village. The most
natural form of the village seems to be that of a colony from
the family, consisting of the children and grandchildren whom
some people describe as 'fellow-sucklings'. This is the reason
why our cities were at first ruled by kings—because the Greeks
were under royal rule before they came together, as the
barbarians still are. Every family is ruled by its eldest member,
and so in the colonies of the family the kingly form of government prevailed because of the kinship of their members. And
this is what Homer means:

'Each one gives law to his children and to his wives.'

For his Cyclopes lived dispersedly, which was the manner in
ancient times. Also this explains why men say that the gods
have a king, because they themselves either are or were in
olden times under kingly rule. For they imagine not only the
forms of the gods but also their manner of life to be like their
own.

When several villages are united in a single complete community, having already attained the limit of virtually total
self-sufficiency, the state comes into being, originating in the
bare needs of life and continuing in existence for the sake of the
good life. And so, if the earlier forms of society are natural, so
is the state, for it is the end of them, and the nature of a thing is
its end. For what each thing is when its growth is fully complete
we call its nature, whether it is a man, a horse or a family.
Again, the object for which a thing exists, its end, is its chief
good; and self-sufficiency is an end and a chief good.

Hence it is clear that the state is a creation of nature and
that man is by nature a political animal. And a man who is by
nature and not merely by fortune without a state is either low
in the scale of humanity or above it;—he is like the

'Clanless, lawless, hearthless one',

whom Homer reviles, for one by nature unsocial is also 'a
lover of war'; we may compare him to an isolated piece at
draughts.

Now why man is more of a political animal than any bee or
any gregarious animal is evident. Nature, as we often say,
makes nothing in vain, and man alone of the animals is
endowed with speech. And while mere voice is simply an indi-

cation of pain and pleasure and is therefore found in other animals (for their nature has been developed so far as to perceive pain and pleasure and to intimate those sensations to one another), the power of speech is intended to set forth the advantageous and the harmful and therefore likewise the right and the wrong. For it is the special characteristic of man in distinction from the other animals that he alone has any sense of good and evil, of just and unjust, and the like, and the association of living beings who possess this sense makes a family and a state.

Further, the state is prior in nature to the family and to each of us individually, since the whole is necessarily prior to the part. For example, when the whole body is destroyed, foot or hand will not exist except in an equivocal sense, like the sense in which one speaks of a hand carved in stone as a hand; for when destroyed the hand will be no better than that. But things are defined by their working and power, so that when they are no longer such as to fulfil their function we ought not to say that they are the same, but only that they have the same name. The proof that the state is a creation of nature and prior to the individual is that the individual, when in isolation, is not self-sufficient, and so he is like a part in relation to the whole. But a man who is incapable of entering into partnership, or who is so self-sufficient that he has no need to do so, must be either a beast or a god; he is no part of a state. A social instinct is implanted in all men by nature, and yet the man who first founded the state was the greatest of benefactors. For man is the best of all animals when perfected, but when separated from law and justice he is the worst of all. For injustice when possessed of weapons is most dangerous, and man is born possessing weapons for the use of wisdom and virtue, which it is possible to use for entirely opposite ends. And so, if he does not have virtue, he is the most unholy and the most savage of animals, and the most full of lust and gluttony. Justice on the other hand is a uniting element in the state, for the administration of justice, which means the determination of what is just, is the principle of order in the political partnership.

(Aristotle, *Politics* 1252ª1–1253ª38)

SLAVERY

Out of a total population at Athens in 431 B.C. estimated at 315,000 (see p. 14 f.), 115,000 were slaves, of whom 65,000 were in domestic work, 50,000 in industry and 10,000 in the mines. Except for this last group who worked in appalling conditions, Athenian slaves enjoyed a fairly tolerable lot, with considerable freedom and protection under the law. It is easy to over-estimate the effect of slavery on Athenian society. It could not properly be regarded as a chief support of the economy which was a simple one, and its existence did not exempt the free citizens from work, though it did allow them a fair amount of leisure. Broadly, slavery at Athens was a humanely conducted institution; it was a Spartan taunt that one could hardly distinguish between slaves and citizens on the streets of Athens.

Slavery still exists in parts of the world, while 'economic slavery' is held by some to be applicable to industrialised society.

Let us first speak of master and slave, taking into account the needs of practical life and also attempting to reach some better theory concerning their relation than we have at present. Some thinkers hold that the role of a master is a science, and that the management of a household, and the mastership of slaves, and the political and royal rule, as I said at the beginning, are all the same. Others assert that the rule of a master over slaves is contrary to nature, and that the distinction between slave and freeman exists by law only, and not by nature; and since it is based on force, it is therefore unjust.

Property is a part of a household and the art of acquiring property a part of household management (for without the necessaries no man can lead the good life or even live at all). And as in the arts which have a definite sphere the proper instruments must be forthcoming if the work is to be accomplished, so it is in the management of a household. Instruments are of various kinds: some are living, others are lifeless; in the rudder the helmsman has a lifeless, in the look-out man, a living instrument; for in the arts the servant is a kind of instrument. Thus also, a possession is an instrument for supporting life. And so in the organisation of the family a slave is a living possession, and property a number of such instruments; and the slave is himself an instrument taking precedence over all other instruments. For if every instrument could carry out its own work, obeying or seeing what to do in advance, like the statues of Daedalus in the story, or the tripods of Hephaestus which the poet says

'entered of their own accord the assembly of the gods';
if thus shuttles wove and quills played harps of themselves, master workmen would not require assistants nor masters slaves. Here, however, we must draw another distinction: the instruments mentioned are instruments of production, whilst a possession is an instrument of action. The shuttle, for instance, is not only of use; something else is made of it, whereas of a garment or a bed we have only the use. Further, as production and action are different in kind and both require instruments, the instruments which they use must similarly differ in kind. But life is doing things, not making things, and so the slave is an assistant in the class of instruments of action.

Again, the term 'possession' is used in the same way as the term 'part'; for the part is not only part of something else, but wholly belongs to it; and this is also true of a possession. The master is only the master of the slave and does not belong to him, while the slave is not only the slave of his master but wholly belongs to him. Hence we see what the nature and office of a slave are. He who is by nature not his own but another's man is by nature a slave; and he may be described as another's man who, being a human being, is also a possession. And a possession may be defined as an instrument of action, separable from its owner.

But we must next consider whether or not anyone exists intended by nature to be a slave, and for whom such a condition is expedient and right, or whether on the contrary all slavery is against nature.

It is not difficult to answer this question on grounds both of reason and of fact. Authority and subordination are not only inevitable but also expedient conditions; from the moment they are born some are marked out for subjection, others for rule.

And there are many varieties both of rulers and of subjects (and that rule is the better which is exercised over better subjects—for instance, it is better to rule over men than over wild beasts; for the work is better which is carried out by better workmen, and when one party rules and another is ruled, there is a work between them); for in every composite thing, where a plurality of parts, whether continuous or discrete, is combined to produce a single common whole, one always finds a ruling and a subject factor. Such a quality exists in living creatures, but not in them only; it originates in the constitution of the universe, and even in things which have no life there is a ruling principle, as in a musical scale. But this matter perhaps belongs to an investigation lying somewhat outside our present scope. Restricting ourselves to the living creature, we note that it consists primarily of soul and body; and of these two, the one is by nature the ruler, and the other the subject. To discover nature's intentions we must study things that are in a natural state, and not in a state of corruption. And so we must study the man who is in the most perfect state of both body and soul, for in him we shall see the true relation of the two—since in those that are bad or are in a bad condition it could seem that the body often rules the soul because of its vicious and unnatural condition. At all events we may firstly observe in living creatures both a despotical and a constitutional rule: the soul rules the body with a despotical rule, whereas the intellect rules the appetites with a constitutional and kingly rule. It is manifest that the rule of the soul over the body, and of the intellect, the part possessing reason, over the emotional part, is natural and expedient; whereas the equality of the two or rule by the inferior is hurtful in every case. The same holds good between men and the other animals: tame animals are superior in their nature to wild animals, and yet it is expedient for all the former to be ruled by man, for this gives them security. Again, the male is by nature superior, and the female inferior; the one rules, and the other is ruled. And this principle necessarily applies to all mankind.

Where, then, there is such a difference as that between soul and body, or between men and animals (as in the case of those whose function is to use the body and from whom this is the best that can be expected), the lower kind are by nature slaves, and it is better for them as for all inferiors that they should be under the rule of a master. For he is by nature a slave who is capable of belonging to another (and that is why he does so belong), and he who participates in reason so far as to apprehend it but not to possess it; whereas the lower animals cannot even understand a principle, but simply obey their instincts. And also the use made of slaves and of tame animals is not very different; bodily service for the necessities of life is provided by both. Nature would like to make the bodies of freemen and of slaves different—the latter strong for necessary service, the other erect and, although useless for such services, useful for a life of citizenship in the arts both of war and peace. But in fact the very opposite happens—that some have the bodies of freemen and others the souls. And certainly, if men differed from one another in the mere forms of their bodies as much as the statues of the gods do from men, everyone would say that those who are inferior should be the slaves of the superior. And if this is true of the body, there is far juster a reason for this rule to be laid down with regard to the soul. But beauty of soul is not so easy to see as beauty of body. It is clear, then, that some men are by nature free, and others slaves, and that for the latter slavery is an institution both expedient and just.

But at the same time it is not hard to see that those who take the opposite view are also right in a manner. The words 'slavery' and 'slave' are employed in two senses. There is a slave or slavery by law as well as by nature. The law of which I speak is a sort of agreement under which whatever is taken in war is said to belong to the conquerors. But this conventional right is arraigned by many jurists even as a statesman is impeached for proposing an unconstitutional measure; they say that it is outrageous that because one man has the power to do violence and has superior strength another should be his slave and subject. Even the learned disagree among themselves on this matter. But the origin of the dispute and what makes the viewpoints overlap is the fact that in a certain manner virtue, when given the means, has actually the greatest power of exercising force; and as superior power only occurs where there is superior excellence of some kind, power seems to imply virtue, and the argument seems to be simply one about justice (for it arises because the one party holds justice and good-will to be identical, while the other identifies it with the mere rule of the stronger). If these views are thus set out separately, the other views have no force or plausibility at all, implying that the superior in goodness has no claim to rule and be master.

But others, clinging, as they think, simply to some principle of justice (for law and custom are a sort of justice), assume that slavery in accordance with the custom of war is justified by law, but at the same moment they deny the assertion. For there is the possibility that wars may be unjust in their origin. Again, no one would ever say that he is a slave who does not deserve slavery; otherwise men of the highest rank would be slaves and the children of slaves if they happened to be taken prisoner and sold. Greeks therefore do not like to call Greeks slaves, but confine the term to barbarians. But, in using this language, they are really referring to the natural slave of whom we spoke at first; for it has to be admitted that some are slaves everywhere, others nowhere. The same applies also about nobility; Greek nobles consider themselves noble not only in their own country but everywhere, but they think that barbarian noblemen are noble only when at home, thereby implying that there are two kinds of nobility and freedom, the one absolute, the other relative, as Helen says in Theodectes:

'But who would dare to call me servant who am on both sides descended from divine stock?'

What else does this mean but that they distinguish freedom and slavery, noble and humble birth, by virtue and vice? For they assume that just as men and brutes beget men and brutes, so also from good parents a good son springs. But though nature may intend this, she cannot always bring it about.

It is clear, then, that there is some reason for this dispute, and that all are not either slaves by nature or freemen by nature, and also that in some instances there is a marked distinction between the two classes, making it expedient and right for the one to be slaves and the other to be masters.

(Aristotle, *Politics* 1253^{b}18–1255^{b}7)

Though admittedly necessary to the state's existence, Aristotle considers tradesmen and craftsmen from the nature of their work to be incapable of achieving political *areté*. Slaves (those 'living tools')

cannot attain *areté* either; but while he proclaims that slavery is
natural (as we have seen), he does not assert that it is necessary for the
state's existence. Aristotle agrees with Plato that the aim of the state
should be not money or wealth but human good, and that political
progress depends not on institutions but on human character. Aristotle
subordinated in his thinking the moral to the intellectual virtues, and
in his denigration of industry and commerce along with Plato (see
p. 48) he was sawing off the branch on which as a leisured *rentier* he
was sitting. Yet these two men had a real point; they were thinking
in terms of a civilised order whose object was not power or money, but
a humane ideal through which men could properly fulfil themselves
as men, and where commerce, if necessary for the moment, was not
the end of life. The Greek economy was simple, the subsistence
standard low; a master did not live in a style utterly different from
that of a slave. The ultimate ideal for human society cherished by
Aristotle (and Plato) gives us, obsessed as we are with questions of
productivity and balance of payments, and hemmed in by an
urbanised and industrialised environment, much matter for thought.
In the quest for continued economic expansion are we overlooking
the deep and lasting values?

THE TYPES OF CONSTITUTION

Let us begin by considering the usual definitions of oligarchy
and democracy, and what justice is under an oligarchy and
under a democracy. For all men cling to justice of some kind,
but they advance only to a certain point and do not express in
its entirety the principle of absolute justice. For instance, it is
thought that justice is equality, and so it is, though not for
everyone but only for those who are equals; and it is thought
that inequality is just, for so it is, though not for everyone, but
for those who are unequal. But the disputants omit the persons,
and so judge wrongly. The reason is that they themselves are
concerned in the decision, and perhaps most people are poor
judges when their own interests are in question. And while
justice implies a relation to persons as well as to things, and a
just distribution implies, as I have already said in the *Ethics*,
the same ratio between the persons and between the things,
they agree about the equality of the things, but dispute about
the equality of the persons, mainly for the reason which I have

just given—because they are poor judges when their own interests are in question; and secondly, because the contending parties advocate a limited and partial justice, but imagine they are maintaining it in the absolute sense. For the one party, if they are unequal in one respect, for instance in wealth, consider that they are unequal in all. And the other party, if they are equal in one respect, for instance free birth, consider that they are equal in all. But they leave out of account the most important point. For if men formed the community and came together for the sake of wealth simply, their share in the state would be proportionate to their property, so that the oligarchical position would appear to be valid—that is, in a partnership with a capital of a hundred minae it would not be just for the man who contributed one mina to have a share either of the principal or the profits equal to that of the man who supplied the whole of the remainder. But a state exists for the sake of a good life, and not for the sake of life only; if life only were the objective, a collection of slaves or lower animals would be a state, but they cannot in fact, for they have no share in happiness or in a life of free choice. Nor does a state exist for the sake of an alliance and protection from injustice, nor again for the sake of exchange and of business relations; for if so, Etruscans and Carthaginians and all those who have commercial treaties with one another would be the citizens of one state. They have, it is true, agreements about imports, and covenants concerning the avoidance of mutual injury, and written articles of alliance. However, they do not have officials in common appointed to enforce their engagements; different states each have their own magistracies. Nor does one state take any concern over the observance of proper moral standards by the citizens of the other, nor see that those who come under the terms of the treaty do no harm or wickedness at all, but only that they do not commit any wrong against each other. On the other hand, all those who are concerned about good government do take civic virtue and vice into consideration. Thus it may further be inferred that virtue must be the concern of a state that is truly so called and not merely enjoys the name; for otherwise the community becomes merely an alliance which differs only in place from alliances of which the members live apart; and law is only a convention, 'a guarantee to one another of justice', as the sophist Lycophron says, and has no power to make the citizens good and just.

The truth of this is obvious; for if we were to bring together the sites of two cities into one, so that the city-walls of Megara and Corinth touched, they would still not be one city, not even if the citizens had the right to intermarry, which is one of the elements of community characteristic of states. And similarly if men lived at a distance from one another, yet not so far apart as to have no intercourse, but had laws to prevent their wronging one another in their interchange of products, neither would this be a state. Let us imagine that one man is a carpenter, another a farmer, another a shoemaker, and so on, and the whole population numbered ten thousand: nevertheless, if they have nothing in common except exchange, alliance, and other such things, that would still not be a state. Why so? Surely not because they are at a distance from one another, for even if such a community were to come together in one place, but each man had a house of his own, which was in a way his state, and they formed an alliance with one another, but only against wrongful aggressors, not even then would they seem to those who consider the matter carefully to constitute a state, if their association with one another was of the same character after as before their union. It is manifest therefore that a state is not a mere society, having a common locality, established for the prevention of mutual injury and for the sake of exchange. These are necessary pre-conditions of a state's existence, but all of them together do not constitute a state, which is a community of families and aggregations of families in well-being, for the sake of a full and self-sufficient life. Such a community can only come into being among those who live in the same place and intermarry. And so there arise in cities family connections, brotherhoods, common sacrifices, amusements which draw people together. But these are created by friendship, for friendship is the motive of social life. While therefore the object of a state is the good life, these things are means to that end. And the state is the union of families and villages in a full and self-sufficient life, by which we mean a happy and honourable life.

Our conclusion, then, is that political society exists for the sake of noble actions, and not of mere companionship. Hence those who contribute most to such fellowship have a larger part in the state than those who have the same or a greater freedom or nobility of birth but are inferior to them in political virtue, or than those who exceed them in wealth but are surpassed by them in virtue.

It is therefore clear from what has been said that all the supporters of different forms of government speak of a part of justice only.

(Aristotle, *Politics* 1280^{a}7–1281^{a}11)

EDUCATION IN THE IDEAL STATE

Civilisation is the life of the mind; material prosperity does not make a nation civilised. Greek thinkers show a striking preoccupation with civilisation and its values. It has been said that a main weakness of our own age is the lack of a definite view of life. Undistracted by the extremes of either poverty or wealth and open to enquiry, the Greeks gave their attention to developing a culture where the emphasis was on self-fulfilment and primal simplicity. Much thought was given to education. A central topic of Plato's *Republic* is the training of the leaders of the ideal state, and Aristotle contributed to the debate—which still goes on. How far should education be regarded as a political issue? What should children be taught to become good citizens? Should we not see education as a life-long process with a moral as well as an intellectual component?

No one would dispute that the education of the young requires the lawgiver's special attention; the neglect of this in states does harm to the constitution. Education ought to be moulded to suit the particular form of government, for each government has its own character which formed it originally and which continues to preserve it. The democratic spirit promotes democracy and the oligarchic oligarchy; and always the better the spirit the better the government.

Moreover, if a faculty or an art is to be exercised previous training and habituation are required—so that clearly this is also necessary for the pursuit of virtue. And since the whole

city has one end it is obvious that education should be one and
the same for all, and that it should be public and not private—
not as it is now when each man superintends his own children's
education, giving them separate instruction of the kind that
seems best to him. But matters of public concern should be
under public supervision. Nor should we think that any of the
citizens belongs to himself, for they all belong to the state and
are, each of them, a part of the state, and the care of the several
parts is bound up with that of the whole. In this regard as in
some others the Spartans deserve praise because they pay the
greatest attention to the training of their children and treat
education as the business of the state.

It is clear, then, that there should be legislation about
education and that it should be conducted on a public system.
But it now remains to consider what the character of this public education should be and how children should be educated.
At present there are disagreements about the subjects, for
people are divided as to what ought to be taught, whether we
look to virtue or to the best life. Nor is it clear whether education should be directed more with regard to intellect than to
character. The prevailing practice is confusing; it is quite uncertain what our guiding principles should be—whether what
is useful in life or virtue or the higher knowledge should be the
object of our training; all three views have been held. Further,
there is no agreement about the means, for different people
proceed from different notions about the nature of virtue and
so disagree about its practice.

It is not therefore hard to see that the young must be taught
those useful arts which are indispensable—but not all useful
arts, for pursuits are divided into liberal and illiberal; and
young children should have imparted to them only such kinds
of knowledge as will be useful to them without rendering them
vulgar. Any pursuit, art or science which makes the body, soul
or mind of free men useless for the employments and actions of
virtue must be considered as vulgar. Hence we call vulgar all
such arts as tend to deform the body, and also the employments
which earn wages since they absorb and degrade the mind.
There are some liberal arts which it is quite fitting for free
men to pursue, but only up to a point, for to devote oneself too

assiduously to them in order to achieve perfection in them is to run the risk of undergoing the injurious results specified. Important too is the aim a man sets himself; if he does or studies anything for his own sake or for that of his friends or with a view to excellence, it is not illiberal, but the man who follows the same pursuit for the sake of others would often appear to be acting in a menial and servile manner. The branches of study established at present are partly liberal and partly illiberal in character, as was said before.

There are perhaps four customary branches of education—(1) reading and writing, (2) gymnastic exercises, (3) music, to which some people add (4) drawing. Reading, writing and drawing are taught as being useful for the purposes of life in a variety of ways, and gymnastics as contributing to manly courage. Concerning music one may feel doubtful—nowadays most people cultivate it for the sake of pleasure, but those who originally included it in education did so because, as has often been said, nature herself requires that we should be able not only to work well but to use our leisure well; for, to speak about it yet again—the first principle of all action is leisure. Both are required, but leisure is better than occupation and is its end; and so the question arises, what is the proper occupation for us when at leisure? Assuredly leisure should not be employed in play since it would follow that play is our end in life. But if this is inconceivable and amusement is needed more in the midst of serious employment than at other times (for the man who is working hard needs relaxation, and amusement provides relaxation, while employment is accompanied by effort and exertion), we should introduce amusements only at suitable times since we are applying them to serve as medicine. For the activity of play is a relaxation of the soul and gives us recreation because of its pleasantness. But leisure itself seems to contain pleasure and happiness and enjoyment of life, which are experienced not by the busy but by the leisured. For the man who is occupied has in view some end which he has not yet achieved; but happiness is an end since all men think it is accompanied by pleasure and not by pain. However, people differ in their definition of this pleasure, each being influenced by his own nature and character. The pleasure of the best man is the best and arises from the noblest sources.

It is therefore clear that there are branches of learning and education which we must pursue merely with a view to leisure spent in intellectual activity, and that these are ends in themselves; whereas the forms of learning related to business are to be seen as necessary and as means to other things. Hence our forefathers included music in education, not on the ground either of its necessity or utility (for there is nothing necessary about it, nor is it useful in the same way as reading and writing which are useful for business and household management, in the acquisition of knowledge and in political life, nor like drawing, useful for making us better judges of the works of artists, nor again like the gymnastic art which gives health and strength). There remains, then, the usefulness of music as a pastime in leisure, which is evidently the purpose for which people actually introduce it, considering it a fit form of pastime for the leisure of free men; as Homer says—

'But him alone it is right to call to the festal banquet', and after these words he speaks of certain others whom he describes as inviting

'The bard who would delight them all'.
And also in another place Odysseus says that there is no better pastime than when men are enjoying good cheer and

'The banqueteers, sitting in due order throughout the hall, hear the voice of the minstrel'.

It is clear, then, that there is a form of education in which parents should train their sons, not because it is useful or necessary but as being liberal and noble. Whether this is of one kind only or of several kinds, and if so, what they are, must be discussed later. But as it is, we are so far forward in our treatment of the question as to be able to say that the ancients provide testimony for us; for their opinion may be gathered from the fact that music is one of the established and traditional branches of education. And it is also clear that some of the useful subjects as well ought to be studied by children not only because of their usefulness, like the study of reading and writing, but also because they may lead on to other branches of knowledge. Similarly they should be taught drawing, not to prevent their making mistakes in their private purchases nor their being cheated in the buying and selling of furniture, but rather because it makes a man observant of the beauty of the human form. To look for utility everywhere is entirely un-suited to those who are great-souled and free.

(Aristotle, *Politics* 1337ª11–1338ᵇ4)

For the approving reference to the Spartans in the second paragraph see p. 11. The word 'liberal' as used by Aristotle here and elsewhere means 'of or pertaining to a free man' (who alone, as opposed to a woman or a slave, was capable or achieving 'virtue'—see p. 43 f.). What might be our own views on the ideal curriculum and on 'training for leisure'? Aristotle thinks of the state as the framework within which the individual citizen may find fulfilment or happiness (cp. p. 34 ff.); here we might consider the comment, 'where a govern-ment decides to ensure not Justice but Happiness for its people, it is on the road to despotism'.

STOIC IDEAS ON THE STATE, FAMILY, INTERNATIONALISM

Cicero's work 'On the Ends of Goods and Evils' (*de Finibus Bonorum et Malorum*, 45 B.C.; usually known simply as *de Finibus*) is a treatise on the theory of ethics, and is part of his programme to introduce Greek philosophical ideas to the Romans, who had no aptitude for abstract speculation, their genius expressing itself rather in action. Other such philosophical writings by Cicero are: 'On the Republic' (*de Re Publica*, 54–51 B.C.), of which only part is extant; five books of 'Tusculan Disputations' (44 B.C.), an imaginary discussion on the subject of the wise man and virtue; 'On the Nature of the Gods' (44 B.C.) in three books; and the three books of the *de Officiis* (44 B.C.), a manual on 'moral duties'.

After Aristotle philosophy tended to become more and more a practical guide to life, the founts of original speculation having dried up. Epicureanism, a system of thought named after its founder Epicurus (died 270 B.C.), made 'pleasure', which was interpreted as absence of pain, its key moral principle; to live quietly amidst like-minded friends, far from the stir and bustle of public activity, was the Epicureans' ideal; politics and anything else likely to upset the soul's tranquillity were to be completely avoided.

In strong contrast, the Stoics' belief in the brotherhood of man (see p. 21) meant for them full involvement in the affairs of society. Since the Macedonian empire under Alexander the Great had absorbed the small independent city-states which Plato and Aristotle knew and which they had regarded as indispensable for the living of the good life, and since thus the division between Greeks and barbarians had been gradually disappearing, the Stoics envisaged a world-city or cosmopolis of which all men were citizens. Stoicism and Epicureanism were contemporary movements; Epicureanism advocated retreat into passive quietism, Stoicism looked outward with impartial benevolence.

Cicero's *de Finibus* consists of three separate dialogues, in which he examines and criticises through the various interlocutors the ethical positions of Epicureanism, Stoicism and the 'Old Academy' of Antiochus, under whom he had studied, 79–78 B.C., and who advanced an eclectic doctrine based on Academic (i.e. Platonic), Peripatetic (i.e. Aristotelian) and Stoic teaching. The following excerpt (3. 62–68) gives some of the main Stoic ideas about the family, the state and internationalism. The speaker is Marcus Cato (95–46 B.C.), politician and great-grandson of Marcus Porcius Cato the Censor (234–149 B.C.) whose moral austerity was proverbial.

The Stoics regard it as important to recognise that nature creates in parents a love for their children; on this love there is founded that social community of the human race to which we afterwards attain. This must be obvious in the first place from the shape of the body and its limbs, which by themselves are sufficient to demonstrate that procreation of offspring is part of nature's plan. But it could not be consistent that nature should both intend offspring to be produced and make no provision for them to be lovingly tended when born. Even in the lower creatures the power of nature can be discerned; when we observe the labour which they expend on bearing and rearing their young, we seem to be listening to the voice of nature herself. And so as it is clear that it is natural for us to shrink from pain, so it is manifest that the impulse to love those whom we have produced comes from nature herself. From this impulse there arises the sense of mutual attraction, itself given to us by nature, which unites human beings; and this impulse entails that through the mere fact of their common humanity one man should feel another man to be his kin. For just as some parts of the body (such as the eyes and ears) are created as it were for their own sakes, while other parts (the legs or the hands, for example) also serve the purposes of the other limbs, so some very large animals are born for themselves alone; whereas the sea-pen, as it is called, in its roomy shell, and the creature named *pinoteres* because it guards the sea-pen, which swims out of the sea-pen's shell, then takes itself back into it and is shut up inside, thus appearing to have given its host warning to be on the look-out—these creatures, along with the ant, the bee, the stork, carry out certain actions for the sake of others besides themselves. The bond of mutual regard amongst human beings is much tighter. It therefore follows that we are fitted by nature to form unions, societies and states.

Further, the Stoics maintain that the universe is governed by divine will; it is a city or state of which both men and gods are members, and each one of us is a part of this universe. And from this it is a natural consequence that we should put the common advantage before our own. For just as the laws set the safety of all before the safety of individuals, so a good, wise and law-abiding man, conscious of his duty to the state, takes thought for the advantage of all more than for that of himself or of any single individual. The person who betrays his country does not deserve more blame than the man who betrays the common advantage or security for the sake of his own advantage or security. This is the reason why praise is due to the one who dies for the commonwealth, because it is proper for us to love our country more than ourselves. And since it is regarded as wicked and inhuman for men to say—the sentiment is usually conveyed in a familiar Greek line—that they do not care whether their deaths are followed by a universal conflagration, it is certainly true that we must take thought for the interest of posterity.

It is from this feeling that the practice of drawing up a will and appointing guardians for one's children when one is dying has arisen. And the fact that no one would willingly pass his life in a desert alone, even though there was an unbounded supply of pleasures to hand, easily shows that we are born for human society and intercourse, and for a natural partnership with our fellow human beings. Further, we are imbued by

nature with the desire to benefit as many people as we can, and
particularly by imparting information and the principles of
wisdom. Hence it would be difficult to find anyone who will not
impart to another any knowledge he himself may have—so
strong is our propensity not only to learn but also to teach. And
just as bulls have a natural instinct to fight with all their
strength and might in defence of their calves against lions, so
those who have great gifts and capacity for service (like
Hercules and Liber in mythology) are by nature impelled to be
the protectors of the human race. Also, when we give Jupiter
the titles of Best and Greatest, of Saviour, Patron of Guests,
Stayer of the Battle-line, what we wish to imply is that the
safety of mankind is in his keeping. But it is quite inconsistent
for us to expect the immortal gods to love and cherish us when
we neglect and despise one another. Therefore, just as we use
our limbs before we have learned for what useful purpose
we have received them, so we are by nature joined together
and allied in the common society of the state. If this were
not so, there would be no room either for justice or benevolence.

But just as the Stoics believe that men are united by the ties
of right, so they consider that no right exists as between man
and beast. For Chrysippus well said that all other things were
created for the sake of men and gods, but that these exist for
the sake of their own mutual fellowship and society, so that
men can make use of beasts for their own purposes without
injustice. And since, he said, the nature of man is such that a
code of law as it were subsists between the individual person
and the human race, he who upholds this code will be just and
he who departs from it unjust. But just as, though the theatre
is a public place, it is still correct to say that the particular seat
a person has taken is his, so in the state or universe, though these
are common to all, no principle of justice opposes the possession by individuals of private property.[1] Again, since we see
that man is born to protect and safeguard his fellow men, it
follows from this natural arrangement that the Wise Man of
Stoicism should wish to take part in politics and government,

[1] For Plato and Aristotle and the question of private property, see p. 80 ff.

and so as to live in accordance with nature to take to himself a wife and desire to have children by her. Even the passion of love when it is pure is not considered by the Stoics to be out of keeping with the character of their Wise Man.

(Cicero, *de Finibus* 3. 62–68)

II. The Individual, the State, Justice and Order

PERICLES' FUNERAL ORATION

Thucydides' method in his history (for which see p. 13) is to deal with his material a year at a time (annalistically), the events of each summer and winter being narrated in order. At intervals he inserts speeches giving, as he says, the substance of what the actual personages could have said. He uses these speeches to make clear the issues at any particular juncture and to comment not only on the situations as they occur but also on the hopes, fears and aspirations of both sides. The celebrated Funeral Oration of Pericles (book 2, chs. 35–46) over those who fell in the first year of the war may well follow the ground-plan of what was actually said and it certainly is in line with other works of this kind which have survived. It is, however, a full statement of the ideals of Periclean Athens—ideals admittedly shot through with élitist assumptions (cp. passage on p. 31 ff. and the introductory remarks on it); a fairly common reproach against classical studies has been that they are concerned with socieities in which a 'snobbish' view of life prevailed, in which a contemptuous attitude was taken up towards anything useful. Such criticism probably applies more to the Greeks than to the Romans, but even so, though there were defects in Greek attitudes and practice, they saw clearly that civilisation is concerned with the human mind, with beauty and truth (cp. introductory comments, p. 47). They were not very rich (as compared with, say, Persia) or very powerful, but they had a vision which showed them that men advanced in civilisation by educating themselves—the word *paedeia* means in Greek both 'education' and 'civilisation'. And in some measure they passed on these ideals to the Romans. How is civilisation viewed today?

We enjoy a form of government which does not copy the laws of our neighbours, but we are rather ourselves a pattern to people than imitators of others. By name, because it is not administered for the benefit of the few but for the many, our constitu-

tion is called a democracy, but with regard to the laws all have
equality as concerns their private differences. With regard to
public rank, in so far as each man has distinction for anything
he is given advancement not so much from consideration of
class as of merit. No one, so long as he has it within him to be of
service to the state, is kept in political obscurity by poverty.
We are liberal in our political life, and this is true also of our
day-to-day life in our relations with one another. We do not
fall out with our next-door neighbour if he enjoys himself in his
own way, nor wear offensive looks on our face which, though
harmless, still hurt people's feelings. We live together harmoniously in private matters; in public matters we keep to the
law because of our respect for it. We are obedient to those we
put in positions of authority, and we obey the laws themselves,
especially those which have been laid down for the sake of the
oppressed and those unwritten laws which it is an acknowledged shame to transgress. . . .

Concerning military security also we differ from our enemies
in these ways. We throw our city open to everyone and never,
by the expulsion of strangers, prevent anyone from either
learning or observing things, the sight of which unconcealed
could confer an advantage on any of our enemies. For we put
our trust not so much in preparations and stratagems as in our
stoutness of heart for daring deeds. As to modes of education,
our opponents aim at acquiring a manly character by labor-
ious training from their very youth, while we, though living
comfortably at ease, go forward no less boldly to meet equal
dangers. A proof of this is the fact that the Spartans never
march against our country by themselves but together with all
their confederates, while we usually conquer without difficulty
in battle upon enemy territory those who are defending their
own possessions. . . .

We cultivate good taste with simplicity and combine culture
with manliness; and we employ our wealth rather as a means
for action than as a subject for boasting. Poverty is nothing
shameful for a man to confess, but not to escape it by effort is
more shameful. In attending to our private affairs we do not
neglect the state, and others who are engaged in business can
still form a sufficient judgment on political matters. For we are

the only people who regard the man who takes no part in these things not as unofficious but as useless. We Athenians, in our own persons, take our decisions on policy or submit them to proper discussions, for we do not look upon words as being incompatible with deeds; the real hindrance lies in hasty action before an issue has been properly debated. For we have this characteristic to a remarkable extent, that we are capable at the same time of taking risks and of assessing them beforehand. Other men are brave through ignorance, and calculation makes them afraid. But those who can most truly be considered courageous are the people who, knowing best what is terrible and what is pleasant in life, nevertheless do not shrink from dangers. With regard to general good feeling we have always differed from most other men, for we make friends not by receiving but by conferring kindness. The one who has conferred the favour is the firmer friend so as to keep alive as due to him the accruing gratitude by the continuation of his goodwill towards him to whom he showed the kindness. But the man who owes gratitude in return is more indifferent in his attitude, knowing that it is not as a favour but as a debt that he will repay the kindness. We are the only people who fearlessly benefit anyone, not so much from calculations of expediency as from the confidence due to our liberal ideas.

In short I declare that our whole city provides a liberal education for Greece, and that, in my opinion, each individual citizen amongst us would prove equal to the most varied circumstances with the utmost grace and versatility. And that this is no mere passing boast so much as actual truth is indicated by the very power of the state, which we have won by such habits. Alone of the states we know, Athens, when brought to the test, turns out superior to what was imagined of her, and in her case alone no invading enemy feels shame at being defeated and no subject has room for finding fault on the grounds that he is governed by a people unworthy of such rule. But we shall be admired both by present and future generations as having exhibited our power with clear proofs and by no means without evidence, and as having no need of Homer to praise us or of anyone else whose poetry might for the moment charm, but whose estimation of facts will fall short of what is true. And we shall be admired for having by our adventurous spirit forced an entry into every sea and land, and for having everywhere established everlasting memorials of our noble acts of valour. It was, then, for such a country that these men, honourably resolving not to have it taken away from them, fell fighting, and it is right that every one of the survivors should be willing to suffer on its behalf.

This is the very reason why I have dilated on the characteristics of the state, seeking to demonstrate that the struggle is not for the same object in our case as in that of people who have none of these advantages in an equal degree, and at the same time to establish clearly by proofs the truth of the eulogy of those men over whom I am now speaking.

(Thucydides 2. 37–41, excerpted)

Pericles' strictures (para. 3) on the poor who make no effort to help themselves call to mind the Victorians' patronising approval of the 'good poor' who 'tried to better themselves'. What causes does modern analysis see as producing poverty?

THE MELIAN DIALOGUE

The island of Melos had not joined the defensive alliance known as the Delian Confederacy (the island of Delos was the seat of the common treasury) which was set up by Athens to preserve Greek independence against Persian encroachments (478–477 B.C.)—see p. 11. The Melians were neutral at the start of the Peloponnesian War, but the Athenian general Nicias attacked them in 426 B.C., and ten years later they were brutally subjugated by the Athenians. In the Debate by which Thucydides dramatises the issue the Athenian emissaries assume confidently that might is right, reminding us of the current *nomos-physis* (convention-nature) controversy—see p. 12. The critics of traditional morals opposed 'nature' to 'convention' or 'custom', asking what rights or justification convention had. Thus all the accepted order of human life was called into question. Plato represents Callicles in his dialogue *Gorgias* and Thrasymachus in the *Republic* (see p. 67) as insisting that the whole of popular morality is a human fiction, with no foundation in nature which in itself knows nothing of right or wrong but recognises only the rights of the stronger. This is the line of argument adopted by the Athenians towards the Melians; they offer them a simple choice between subjection or destruction, and they are totally unaffected by the islanders' arguments. We give the Debate in full; in reflecting on it one might consider where the basis of morality lies. Do good morals, in other words, begin with right attitudes to others?

Athenians: If you have come to this meeting to argue upon suspicions about the future, or if you have come for any other reason except to face facts and on the basis of them see how you can save your city, then we can see no point in continuing. But if you are going to do as we suggest, then we shall speak.

Melians: It is natural and pardonable for men in our position to have recourse to many kinds of argument and different viewpoints. However, you are correct in saying that this meeting is taking place with a view to our preservation, and the discussion can proceed, if you will have it so, along the lines you propose.

Athenians: Then we for our part shall use no fine phrases saying, for instance, that as the conquerors of the Persians we have a right to empire or that we are now coming against you because we are being injured—this would be a long speech that no one would find credible. Nor do we want you on your side to think that you will influence us by saying that though you were their colony you did not join the Spartans, or that you have never done us any harm. But we advise you to try to get what you can get, taking into consideration what we both really do think. For you know as well as we do that, where practical men talk about these matters, the standard of justice depends upon the equality of power to compel and the strong do what they have the power to do, while the weak accept what they must.

Melians: Then in our opinion at any rate (since you have forced us to speak of self-interest and leave justice out of account) it is useful that you should not destroy a principle that is to the common good—namely, that all those who fall into danger should be treated fairly and justly, and that such people should be allowed to employ and profit by arguments that fall short of strict accuracy. And this is a principle that is not less in your interest since your fall would attract the most dreadful vengeance and would be an example to the rest of mankind.

Athenians: We for our part are not anxious about the outcome should our empire come to an end. Apprehension arises not so much over being conquered by a state which rules others, as Sparta does (though our present debate is not concerned with Sparta), as from the possibility of our subjects in any quarter by themselves attacking and overwhelming those who have had rule over them. So far as this matter is concerned the danger may be left to us to face. What we shall show you now is that we are here for the benefit of our empire and that what we are going to say is for the preservation of your state. For we wish to have you in our empire without any trouble and to have you preserved for the advantage of us both.

Melians: How, then, could it prove just as advantageous for us to be slaves as for you to be masters?

Athenians: You by submitting would save yourselves from suffering disaster, while we would gain by not destroying you.

Melians: You would accept that we be neutral, friends instead of enemies and allied to neither side?

Athenians: No, because it is not so much your hostility which is hurtful to us; it is rather the case that if we were on friendly terms with you our subjects would regard it as a sure sign of weakness in us, whereas your hatred is evidence of our power.

Melians: Is that your subjects' idea of fair play—to regard as on the same footing people who are not at all connected with you and those who, being mostly your colonists or else rebels, have been reduced to subjection by you?

Athenians: So far as right and wrong are concerned they think that there is no difference between the two, that those who still keep their independence do so because they are strong, and that if we abstain from attacking them it is because we are afraid. And so, by conquering you we shall not only have a greater empire but a more secure one too. We have command of the sea, while you are islanders, and weaker islanders too than others; and so it is of special importance that you do not escape.

Melians: But do you think there is no security in what we suggested? For here again, as you have excluded us from appeals to justice and urge us to yield to considerations of your advantage, we too must explain what is expedient for us, and, if yours and ours happen to coincide, we must try to persuade you of the fact. For how can you avoid making enemies of all states that are at present neutral, when they see what is happening here and naturally reckon that in due course you will attack them too? Does this not mean that you are strengthening your present enemies and forcing others to become your enemies against their will and intention?

Athenians: We are not in fact so much afraid of mainland states. Having their liberty, they will long delay before they begin to take precautions against us. We are more anxious about islanders like yourselves, who are anywhere unsubdued, and those who by the severity of our rule are becoming embittered against us. These are the people who would most give way to recklessness and bring both themselves and us into the most obvious danger.

Melians: Surely, then, if you run such a risk so as to retain your empire and your subjects so as to escape from it, we who are still free would show great weakness and cowardice if we failed to face up to everything that comes rather than submit to slavery.

Athenians: No; not at least if you take a sensible view of the case. This is no fair contest, with honour on one side and shame on the other. You are rather deliberating about your preservation, to avoid resisting those who are far too strong for you.

Melians: Yet we know that in war fortune sometimes makes the odds more even than could have been expected from the different numbers on each side. And so far as we are concerned, to yield is to give up hope immediately, whereas by making an effort there is still hope that we may yet stand upright.

Athenians: Hope, the bringer of solace in danger, when entertained by those who have solid advantages behind them, though it may injure still does not ruin them. But hope is by nature a costly thing, and those who risk their all upon one cast find out what it means when they are already undone; it does not fail them during the time when the possession of such knowledge would enable them to take precautions. Do not, then, weak as you are and hanging on a single turn of the scale, let this happen to you. And do not try to resemble the greater part of mankind who, when they could have saved themselves by human means, after clear and distinct hopes have failed them in their distress, turn to what is blind and vague, to prophecies and oracles and such things which by encouraging hope in men's breasts bring them to destruction.

Melians: It is difficult (and you may be assured that we know it) for us to oppose your power and fortune, unless we are able to do it on equal terms. However, we trust that the gods will give us fortune as good as yours, because we are standing up in a righteous cause against unjust opponents. As for our deficiency in power, we trust that it will be made up for by our alliance with the Spartans, who are bound, if for no other reason, then for the sake of honour and kinship, to assist us. And so our confidence is not so irrational as you assume.

Athenians: As regards the favour of the gods, we think we shall have as much of a share in it as you. Our aims and our actions are completely consistent with mankind's beliefs about the gods and with the principles that men follow in the conduct of their lives. For of the gods we hold as a matter of opinion, and of men we know as a certainty that, following an irresistible instinct, they always maintain their dominion wherever they are the stronger. And we neither enacted this law nor were the first to carry it out when enacted; but having received it when already in force, we merely avail ourselves of it and shall leave it to exist for ever amongst those who come after us. We know that both you and others, if raised to the same power, would do the same. And so, with regard to the gods, we are with good reason unafraid of defeat. But with regard to your views about Sparta which make you confident that she will come to your assistance out of a sense of honour, while we congratulate you on your simplicity, we do not envy your folly. Where they themselves are concerned or the institutions of their country the Spartans are to a quite remarkable degree good. As to their relations with others, though we could descant at length on their behaviour, the matter can be expressed shortly and clearly in this observation, that of all people we know the Spartans are most notable for believing that what is pleasant to them is honourable and that what is expedient is just. And such a view of things is not going to help you in your present unreasonable quest for safety.

Melians: But this is the very ground on which we can feel most secure—their own sense of self-interest which will make them unwilling to abandon their own colonists, the Melians, since that would mean losing the confidence of their friends among the Greeks and helping their enemies.

Athenians: You appear to overlook the fact that the pursuit of self-interest makes people want to be safe, whereas justice and honour involve danger. And where danger is concerned the Spartans are the least daring as a rule.

Melians: But we believe that they would even endanger themselves for our sake and would consider the risk more worth taking than in the case of others, because we lie so close to the Peloponnese that they could carry out operations more easily, while we are more to be trusted than another party would be since we are of the same race and share the same outlook.

Athenians: Yes, but goodwill on the part of those seeking help does not mean safety for the prospective ally. What is important is much greater superiority in power for action; and the Spartans look to this point even more than the rest of the world. Certainly they mistrust their own native resources so much that it is only in company with a great army of allies that they attack a neighbour. It is therefore hardly likely that they, while we are in control of the sea, will cross over to an island.

Melians: But they could still send others. The Cretan sea is a wide one and to intercept a party in crossing it is more difficult for those who control it than to escape is for those who wish to avoid observation. Besides, if they were to fail in this, they would turn against your own land and against such of your allies as Brasidas did not reach. Thus, you will have to exert yourselves, not so much about a country that has nothing to do with you as about trouble nearer home, among your allies and in your own country.

Athenians: On this point you as well as others may learn by actual experience and not remain ignorant that from no single siege did the Athenians ever yet retreat through fear of others. But it strikes us that, though you said you would discuss how you could ensure your own preservation, in all this long conference you have advanced absolutely nothing which could justify people in thinking that they could be preserved. Your chief points are concerned with what you hope may happen in the future, while your present resources are too scanty, compared with those already lined up against you, to give you a chance of survival. You therefore will show a massive lack of common sense if, after asking us to withdraw from this meeting, you still do not come to some conclusion wiser than what you have so far put forward. You will surely not allow yourselves to be led astray by a false sense of honour, which often ruins men when they are confronted by an obvious danger which touches their pride. For in the case of many men, though they all the time foresee the dangers into which they are running, this thing called dishonour, by the influence of a seductive name, lures them on, enslaved as they are to the word, so that they fall voluntarily into irretrievable disasters, incurring dishonour which is all the more dishonourable since it has arisen from their own folly rather than misfortune. You, if you take the correct view, will be careful to avoid this. You will see nothing discreditable in submitting to the greatest of the Greek states when it offers you fair terms—alliance on a tribute-paying basis along with the enjoyment of your own country. And when you are given the choice between war and safety you will avoid taking through arrogance what for you is the worse course. The safest way is to stand up to one's equals, to show deference towards one's superiors, and to act with moderation towards one's inferiors. Think it over, then, when we have retired, and reflect again and again that you are deliberating on the fate of your country, that you have only one country, and that this one single decision you are going to make will affect it for good or ill in the future.

The Athenians then withdrew from the discussion; and the Melians, having been left to themselves, came to a conclusion which was very nearly the same as they had maintained in their previous replies. The following was their answer:
Melians: Our attitude, Athenians, is just the same as it was at

first. We are not prepared to rob in a short moment our city of
the liberty which it has enjoyed for seven hundred years since
its foundation. We put our trust in the fortune which, by the
favour of heaven, has preserved it up to now, and in the help of
man—that is, of the Spartans. In this way we shall try to save
ourselves. But we propose to you that we be your friends and
the enemies of neither side; and that after making a treaty
which shall be agreeable to both you and us, you leave our
country.

This was the reply of the Melians, and the Athenians, just as
they were breaking off the discussion, said:

Athenians: Well then, judging by this decision of yours, you
seem to us unique in your capacity to consider the future as
more certain than what is before your very eyes, and to regard
what is uncertain as a present reality simply because you wish
it were so. As you have staked most on, and trusted most in,
Spartans, luck and hopes, you will in all these things also be
most disappointed.

(Thucydides 5. 87–113)

The Athenians began to lay siege to Melos. They were not at first
successful, but eventually the Melians were forced to surrender un-
conditionally, and the Athenians 'killed all the men of military age
whom they took, and sold the women and children as slaves' (Thucydides *ibid.*, 116).

PLATO ON THE STATE

Plato (427–348/7 B.C.) had seen the failure of democracy in Athens
(see p. 24); but the excesses of the Thirty Tyrants—who seized and
held power for a year (404–403 B.C.) immediately after the end of the
Peloponnesian War and of whom one of the leaders was Plato's
relative Critias—gave him a strong distaste for oligarchy as practised
at Athens. Under the restored democratic government of Thrasybulus
and his colleagues and successors he led a quiet life, teaching and
pursuing his theories. Politics was a life-long interest, and his political
ideals were clearly influenced by Sparta in particular (see p. 11). His
masterpiece, the *Republic*, which is in ten books, opens with Socrates
paying a visit to the aged Cephalus at the Piraeus; he falls into discussion on the nature of justice with Cephalus, then with his son

Polemarchus, and lastly with the eminent Sophist Thrasymachus of Chalcedon.

A chief mark of the Sophists (see p. 12) was a challenging scepticism. Their stress was on practical and readily applied knowledge, their aim being to dispense efficiency, especially in the inter-connected areas of politics and public speaking (for political success depends upon the power of persuasive speech). The whole philosophical atmosphere of Athens after the middle of the fifth century B.C. was permeated by profound scepticism; faith in the possibility of absolute knowledge had been severely shaken since thinkers had questioned both the accuracy of the senses as conveyors of knowledge and the unity and stability of the universe. If in the realm of the physical nothing is fixed and certain, if hot and cold, sweet and sour, do not refer to something objective and permanent but only to the individual's transient sensations, what about the realm of conduct? By the same token were not right and wrong, justice and injustice, merely subjective conceptions with no root in reality? It was to the defeat of this sterile scepticism that Socrates, Plato and Aristotle devoted their intellectual energies.

When Thrasymachus in Republic I (338c) asserts that 'justice is nothing other than that which is advantageous to the stronger', he is arguing along lines not unfamiliar to the age, as the Melian Debate (p. 59 ff.). shows. There seemed to many to be no objective standards to govern the relationship of man to man.

To answer Thrasymachus Socrates himself attempts to define justice and, in order to do so, starts by considering the state, in which he suggests the individual can be seen in magnified form. (While Plato is careful over setting and characterisation, his 'Socrates' must only to a limited extent be an impersonation of the original figure, for the dialogues show a growth in the appreciation of philosophical difficulties and in general intellectual scope which can be attributed only to development in Plato's own thought.) The enquiry includes examination of various kinds of states and of how one kind is the product of another (e.g. tyranny of democracy). The ideal polity is an aristocracy of law-givers trained by philosophical studies and practical experience, with a powerful military caste to provide the common-wealth's defence. Conservatism is a dominant note, political change being seen as something usually injurious; and religion, education and art are generally to be directed by the rulers in accordance with what they know to be for the subjects' good (for the division of society in Plato's ideal state see p. 13 f.). The Spartan consitution (for Plato, Aristotle and Sparta see p. 11) was the model in many of the details of this scheme; the collapse of democratic government at Athens because of its various weaknesses caused Plato to look to the Dorian form of polity in which rigorous authoritarianism suppressed or controlled potentially dangerous individualist tendencies. But we must avoid misunderstanding; the charge of totalitarianism has been too readily flung at Plato. The third and lowest (and largest) class after the law-givers and protectors is not to be confused with the proletariat as it figures in Marxist discussions today. It is the only class allowed by Plato to own private wealth. The selfish scramble for enrichment was one of the great curses of political life for Plato: the dire results of such activity were evident in the obviously corrupt democracy of his own day. Political and economic power were to be completely sundered. 'Good men will not consent to hold office for the sake either of money or honour' (*Rep.* 1.347b). Those who wished to amass a fortune were free to occupy themselves with trade in the third order of society, leaving government to those who were fired by a single ambition—to rule well. For the rulers themselves Plato prescribes common ownership of property and common messes after the Spartan fashion. The possibility of satisfying material greed was not to be an allurement to seek office.

Justice in the state, then, according to Plato is that disposition by which each citizen performs his proper function and each class is content to leave the others alone and pursue its own concerns. This view of the state is applied to the individual person in whom, the soul being considered to have three parts, the mind or rational part is equated with the law-givers or rulers of the state; the 'spirited part' (which refers to the emotions and ambitions) with the protectors or military class; and the appetitive part with the productive workers. Justice in the individual is a condition of inner harmony where the parts make their own contribution to the well-being of the whole. The mind is in control, with the strong driving emotions acting in support, and the various appetites are allowed satisfaction but are yet kept within bounds. Justice is the right integration and balance of the individual's personality under the mind's direction. Plato held the rational part of the soul alone to be immortal.

By this notion of immortality the possibility of knowledge was made real for Plato. Knowledge was recollection. He held that in the unseen world there are laid up patterns or forms or 'ideas' of which everything in this world is a shadowy and imperfect copy. The rational part of the soul, being not only immortal but pre-existent, has a view of the forms in the other world, but forgets what it saw before being embodied in flesh. During its earthly experiences it is gradually reminded of the forms by observing their incorporation in the particular things experienced. The forms have their own hierarchy, the 'idea of the Good' being the supreme one on which all the others depend. The dialogues *Phaedo*, *Phaedrus* and *Meno* contain myths symbolically setting forth this teaching, while the *Republic* itself ends with the Myth of Er on the same theme.

Plato earnestly sought to vindicate the claims of philosophy as a guide to absolute truth and the good life against the sophistic scepticism of his time which was so often expressed in flamboyant and specious language. But his individual-state analogy is open to question.

Plato clearly saw that the thinker can be a man of action and that the man of action ought to be a thinker. Does he argue convincingly for the 'philosopher as king'? We might also consider this remark: 'For Plato, man was to be guided, not by this private conscience, but by Reason, and against Reason there are *no* natural rights.'

Unless philosophers rule as kings in cities, or those who are now called kings and princes become genuine and adequate philosophers, and political power and wisdom meet in one, and those commoner natures who at present pursue either to the exclusion of the other, are forcibly debarred from this behaviour, cities will never have respite from their troubles, nor humanity either, I believe; nor will this constitution which we have just described in our argument come to the fulfilment that is possible for it and see the light of day. . . .

Then are they any better than blind who are completely destitute of the knowledge of things as they really are, who have no distinct pattern in their soul, and are unable like a painter to look at the absolute truth, and continually refer to it, and by their perfect vision of the other world to establish on earth ideals of beauty, justice and goodness or, if established, to guard and preserve them? And shall we appoint them as our guardians rather than those who have come to know every reality, and who are in no way their inferiors in experience or any other part of virtue? Let us discuss, then, how far they can combine both qualifications. We must first ascertain what the philosophic nature is, and, after doing that, we shall then acknowledge, I fancy, that such a union of qualifications is possible, and that they, and they alone, ought to be rulers in the state in whom they are united.

Concerning philosophic natures we may surely agree that they always love that kind of knowledge which reveals to them the eternal realities which are exempt from being driven to and fro by generation and decay. And let us further agree that they are lovers of reality as a whole; there is no part, greater or less, or more or less honourable, which they are willing to renounce, and in this they are like lovers or ambitious men. And if they are to be what we were describing, they must have in their nature this further quality—truthfulness, which is a determination never voluntarily to receive what is false, but to hate it and love the truth. Is there anything more akin to wisdom than truth? Can the same nature be a lover of wisdom and a lover of falsehood? If not, the true lover of learning must from his earliest years strive with all his heart after all truth?

But then, as we know from experience, whenever a man's desires flow in full current in one direction, they will, like a stream which has been drawn off into another channel, be weaker in others; and when a man's desires are drawn towards the sciences and all learning he will be absorbed in the pleasures of the soul, and will desert the pleasures that come through the body—that is, if he is a true philosopher and not a sham one. He will certainly be temperate and in no way covetous; he is the last man in the world to pursue eagerly those aims for the sake of which people love wealth and lavish expenditure.

Another point arises in our consideration of the philosophic nature. There must be no secret inclination to meanness in it. For smallness is surely the most inappropriate quality for a soul which is ever longing after the whole of things. And how can one who has greatness of mind and the power of looking out over all time and all being attach any importance to our human life or regard death as anything to be feared? Thus a cowardly and mean nature will probably have no participation in true philosophy.

Further, can a man who is harmoniously constituted, who is neither covetous nor mean, nor a coward nor a boaster, be by any possibility hard to deal with or unjust? . . .

He who truly keeps his mind fixed upon reality has surely no leisure to look down upon the affairs of earth, to fight and become full of malice and hate; his gaze is always directed towards a fixed and unchanging world where nothing does or suffers injustice and all is governed by order and reason. This world he imitates, and he conforms himself to it as far as possible. A man surely cannot help imitating that with which he lovingly associates. The philosopher in his association with the divine order becomes orderly and divine, as far as mortal may; but like everyone else he will have his detractors. And if he is forced to model not only himself but human nature at large, whether in states or individuals, in accordance with his heavenly vision, do you think he will be an unskilful artist of temperance and justice and every virtue of the people? And if the world perceives that what we are saying about him is true, will they be annoyed with philosophy? Will they disbelieve us when we tell them that no state will ever know happiness unless its draughtsmen are artists who have as their pattern the divine? . . .

Our kind of rulers must be lovers of their country, tried by the test of pleasures and pains, and neither amidst hardships nor in dangers nor at any other critical juncture must they prove unfaithful; the man who fails must be rejected, but the one who always emerges unsullied, like gold tried in the fire, is to be made ruler, and privileges and rewards are to be his in life and after death. Previously I hesitated to make the bold utterance that I am now ready to make—that we must make our most perfect guardians philosophers. Do not imagine that there will be many of them—naturally not; for the gifts which we considered necessary very seldom grow together, being mostly found scattered in bits and pieces. Sharp intelligence, memory, sagacity, cleverness, and similar qualities, together with spirit and high-mindedness, are, as you know, not often found along with the disposition to live a sober, quiet and settled life. Men with these gifts are driven this way and that by their vivacity, and they lose their stability. On the other hand, those steadfast natures which cannot easily be changed from their purpose, which are trusted and employed with confidence, and which in war are impregnable to fear, are equally immovable when there is anything to be learned. They are as slow to move and to learn as though they were torpid, and are apt to yawn and fall asleep over any intellectual toil. Yet we affirm that the guardians must partake of both these sets of qualities in full and fair measure, or else have no share in the highest education, nor in honour nor office. But such people are rare. And so the future ruler must not only be tested in those labours and dangers and pleasures which we have described, but there is something else which we omitted—we must exercise him also in many kinds of studies to see whether the soul will be able to endure the highest studies of all or whether it will flinch as others flinch in other trials.

(Plato, *Republic* 5.473c–e; 484c–486b; 500b–d; 503)

PLATO ON DEMOCRACY

The first paragraph is a critical sketch which is really concerned with Athens. The state where wisdom directed towards the highest and noblest ends holds sway is Plato's ideal. In the Athenian democracy the only ideal is freedom. By 'captain' he means the electorate. With reference to Plato's comments on the weaknesses of Athenian democracy we may consider the remark: 'Freedom versus order is one of the oldest of all political antagonisms and today it is the very heart of politics.'

Imagine something of this kind happening in a ship or a fleet. The captain is bigger and stronger than all the crew, but rather deaf and shortsighted. His seamanship is as defective as his hearing. The sailors are quarrelling about the navigation. Each man thinks he ought to navigate, though up to that time he has not studied the art and cannot give the name of his instructor or the time of his apprenticeship. They go further and assert that it cannot be taught, and they are ready to cut to pieces anyone who says the opposite. They crowd round about the solitary captain, begging and beseeching him to entrust them with the helm. Sometimes if they do not succeed in persuading him but others have their way, they kill those others or throw them overboard, overpower the noble captain with drink or some narcotic, and mutiny, taking over the ship, and make free with the stores, and so drinking and feasting they proceed on their voyage just as one would expect.

Anyone who encourages them and cleverly helps them in their
scheme for taking the ship out of the captain's hands into their
own whether by force or persuasion they compliment with the
name of sailor, pilot, skilled seaman, and they abuse those who
assume a different attitude and call them useless. So far as the
true pilot is concerned, they have no notion that he must pay
attention to the year and the seasons and sky and stars and
winds, and whatever else belongs to his art, if he intends to be
really qualified for the command of a ship, and that he must
and will be the steersman whether people like it or not—such a
combination of authority with the steersman's art they do not
believe possible. Now in ships which are in a state of mutiny
like this do you not think that the true pilot would certainly be
called a star-gazer and a useless babbler by the crews? . . .

(*This next paragraph ironically touches on individualism as a grave weakness in democracy; when each man wants to do as he likes the fabric of the state
is damaged.*)

First of all the citizens are free, the city is full of liberty and
freedom of speech—you may do and say what you like there.
Where the permissive principle rules, the individual is clearly
able to arrange his own life to suit himself. And so in this kind
of state there will be the greatest variety of human character.
It will turn out to be the fairest of constitutions—like a
coloured dress embroidered with every kind of flower, this
constitution will be variegated with every character and be
most beautiful. And just as women and children admire many-
coloured things, so perhaps many people will judge this state
to be fairest of all. And it certainly is the right kind of place in
which to look for a constitution; because of the liberty that
prevails there, it has every kind of constitution. Anyone who
wishes to found a state as we have been doing ought to step
into the democratic city as he would into a bazaar that sells
constitutions and pick out the one that suits him; then, when
he has made his choice, he may found his state. And in this
state there is no need for you to govern even if you have the
capacity, or to be governed if you do not wish to be, or to go to
war when the rest go, or to be at peace when the rest are if you
do not desire to. If there is a law forbidding you to be a magis-

trate or judge, that is no reason why you should not be both magistrate and judge if you have a mind to. Is not this a way of life which for the moment is supremely delightful? Then think of the considerateness of democracy, and its lackadaisical attitude to trifles, and its disregard of all the fine principles which we solemnly laid down at the founding of the city—as when we said that, except for an unusually gifted nature, there never will be a good man who has not right from childhood been used to play amidst beautiful things and make all such things the object of his concern—how sublimely does it trample under foot all these fine principles of ours, utterly indifferent as to what life a man has led before he enters politics, and ready to honour the one who professes to be the friend of the multitude. These and other related characteristics are typical of democracy, a charming form of government, with no rulers and plenty of variety, dispensing its peculiar kind of equality to equals and unequals alike. . . .

(Popular suffrage and the system of election by lot are satirically attacked in the following excerpt. Where is the sense, Plato asks, in deciding the most complicated and crucial issues with reference to public opinion?)

Let us return once more to our favourite images which we use in discussing kingly rulers—the noble captain of a ship and the physician 'who is worth as much as many others put together'. Let us see in them an analogy to politics. Everyone will reflect that we are most terribly treated by them. The physician saves any he wishes to save, and maltreats any he wishes to maltreat, cutting and cauterising and at the same time ordering us to bring him fees, as though exacting tribute, little or nothing of which is spent on the patient, the greater part being consumed by the doctor and his servants. And finally he is bribed by the patient's relatives or enemies and actually brings about his death. And the captains of ships do the same sort of things on innumerable occasions; they deliberately act deceitfully and leave us ashore when the hour of sailing comes; they cause mishaps at sea and cast away their freight, and are guilty of other wrongdoings.

Now suppose that we, bearing all this in mind, were to determine, after consideration, that we would no longer allow either of these arts to rule, without control, over slaves or free men, but that we would call an assembly either of all the people or of the rich only, and that anyone, whether engaged in some other form of skilled labour or without any special qualifications, should be free to offer an opinion about navigation and diseases, how drugs and surgical or medical instruments should be applied to the patients, and how ships should be handled and nautical instruments used and how dangers should be met, not only those of winds and seas that affect the voyage itself, but also those met in encounters with pirates, and if battles have to be fought between men-of-war; and that whatever the majority decided about these matters, whether any physicians or ship captains or merely unskilled persons took part in the deliberations, should be inscribed in the statute-book or adopted in unwritten form as national customs—that henceforth forever ships shall be navigated and the sick cared for in accordance with these principles.

What an absurd notion you have suggested!

And suppose that rulers of the people (our captains and physicians) are appointed annually, either from the rich or from the whole people, on the principle that whoever is chosen by lot should rule; and that after their election they navigate ships and treat the sick according to the written rules.

This is even harder to imagine.

But hear what follows: when their year of office has passed, there will have to be courts of review[1] for our captains and physicians to attend, in which the judges are chosen by lot either from a selected list of the rich or from the whole people; and anyone who pleases may be their accuser, and may lay a charge against them, that during the past year they have not navigated their vessels or treated their patients according to the letter of the law and the ancient customs of their ancestors; and if anyone is found guilty, some of the judges must fix what his punishment or fine shall be.

Surely anyone who consents voluntarily to hold office under such conditions would richly deserve any penalty that might be imposed.

[1] The reference is to the scrutiny of magistrates' performance by special commissioners at the end of their term of office.

Further, if anyone is found investigating the art of pilotage or navigation or the subject of health and true medical doctrine about winds and things hot and cold, contrary to the written rules, or to be indulging in any speculation whatever on such matters, we shall have to enact that he is not to be called a physician or ship captain but a star-gazing kind of loquacious sophist; further, anyone who is properly qualified may bring a charge against him and hale him into court on the ground that he is a corrupter of the young by persuading them to attempt the arts of navigation and medicine in opposition to the laws and to assume arbitrary authority over their patients or ships; and if he is found to be persuading any, whether young or old, to act contrary to the written law, he shall suffer the most extreme penalties. For no one, they say, should presume to be wiser than the laws; every one, it will be said, knows the principles of health and piloting and navigation, for anyone can learn the written laws and ancestral customs in these subjects. If this was the attitude we applied to these sciences, and to strategy ... and any sort of handicraft, or agriculture and planting—what, I ask, would be the result if our practice in all these activities was governed by written regulations and not by knowledge?

Clearly all the arts would be utterly ruined and lost beyond recall because there was a law prohibiting any research into them. And human life, which is hard enough now, would then become absolutely unendurable.

(Plato, *Republic* 488–489a; 557b–558c; *Politicus* 297e–299e)

SUPREME LAW

In the first Cicero passage (from his dialogue *De Legibus*, 'On the Laws') the notion of natural law on which Stoicism laid great stress is considered: above and beyond ordinary human legal codes there was an eternal law. The Stoics argued that, partaking as they do in the divine reason which governs the whole universe, men have been able to apprehend this law and it is the basis of morality and the sound ordering of society; this law is part of the very nature of the world, and is not a mere matter of convention (cp. pp. 51 ff. and 59 ff.). All

men are brothers through their divine kinship and all are citizens of
the world (see p. 21).

But the most foolish notion of all is to imagine that everything
found in the customs or laws of nations is just. Would that be
true, even if the laws had been laid down by tyrants? If the
famous Thirty Tyrants had wished to enact laws at Athens,
or if the Athenians as a whole were delighted by the tyrants'
legislation, surely that would not be sufficient justification for
regarding those laws as just. No more, in my opinion, should
that law be thought just which a Roman vice-consul proposed,
to the effect that a dictator[1] might with impunity kill any
citizen he wished, even without a trial. For justice is one; by it
human society is bound together and it is based on one Law,
which is right reason applied to command and prohibition.
Whoever does not know this Law, whether it has been recorded
in writing anywhere or not, is a man lacking justice.

But if justice is conformity to written laws and national
customs, and if, as the Epicureans say, everything is to be
measured by the standard of utility, then anyone who thinks it
will be a profitable course for him will, if he can, disregard and
violate the laws. Thus it follows that justice does not exist at all,
if it does not exist in nature, and if that part of it which is based
on utility can be subverted by that very utility. And if nature is
not going to be the firm foundation of justice, all the virtues
on which society depends will be destroyed. For where, then,
will there be a place for generosity, or love of country, or
loyalty, or the inclination to be of service to other people or to
show gratitude for benefits received? For these virtues arise
from our natural instinct to love our fellow-men, which is the
foundation of justice. Otherwise, not only consideration for
men but also rites and pious observances in honour of the gods
are destroyed; for these, I believe, ought to be maintained,
not through fear, but because of the close relationship which
exists between man and God.

(Cicero, *De Legibus* 1.42–3)

[1] A *dictator* at Rome was a magistrate with unlimited power appointed in
great emergencies, and superseding the ordinary magistrates.

(The argument of the preceding passage is completed: the natural law is of divine origin.)

True law is right reason in agreement with nature; it is of universal application, constant and everlasting; it summons to duty by its commands, and averts from wrongdoing by its prohibitions. And it does not lay its commands or prohibitions upon good men in vain, though neither have any effect on the wicked. It is a sin to alter this law, nor is it allowable to attempt to repeal any part of it, and it is impossible to abolish it entirely. We cannot be released from its obligations either by senate or people, nor do we require to look beyond ourselves to find an expounder or interpreter of it. Nor will there be any one law at Rome and another at Athens, nor one law now and a different one in the future, but one eternal and unchangeable law will be valid for all nations and all times, and there will be one master and ruler over us all—God; for he is the author, the promulgator, the proposer of this law. If anyone disobeys it, he will be fleeing from himself and denying his human nature and by reason of this very fact he will pay the worst penalties, even if he escapes what is usually considered punishment.

(Cicero, *De Re Publica* 3.22)

(Love as the binding force in society is the theme of this third extract.)

Of all motives none is better adapted to secure a position of power and retain it than love; nothing is more unfavourable to that objective than fear. The poet Ennius has put it excellently:
'The man whom they fear they hate. And when one hates a man, one hopes for his death.'
And recently, with the assassination of our tyrant, Julius Caesar, we discovered (if it was not recognised before) that no amount of power can withstand the hatred of the many. The death of Caesar, whose yoke the state endured under the constraint of arms and to whom, though he is dead, it is still subservient, illustrates how powerful a destructive force is the hatred of men; and the same point is made by the similar fate of all other tyrants, of whom practically no one has escaped such a death. For fear is a poor guardian of lasting power, while on the other hand good will is a sure guarantor even of its permanence.

But granted that severity must be employed by those who keep subjects under control by force—by masters, for example, towards their servants, if they cannot otherwise be held in check; those however who in a free state set out to make themselves feared are without equals in madness. For though the laws have been overwhelmed by some one individual's ascendancy, and though the spirit may have been intimidated, they still sooner or later assert themselves either as a result of the silent verdict of the people or the secret choice of the ballot. Freedom for a while suppressed has sharper fangs than freedom never endangered. Let us therefore embrace the principle which is of the widest application and provides the strongest guarantee not only of security but also of influence and power— that is, to banish fear and hold fast to love.

(Cicero, *De Officiis* 2.34–4)

III. The Individual, the State and Property

Plato suggests that his ruling class should have wives and property in common, by which he hopes that any tendency in them to selfishness will be finally vanquished. Plato's communism, which he himself recognised as visionary and unworkable, bears no relation to the communist creed as understood or practised today, but it does invite comparison with the ideal of the medieval religious orders. In this context, would you agree that 'private property is a corner-stone of civilisation'? And would you agree that 'our possessions may be defended by force but not our beliefs'?

Can we mention any greater evil in a state than discord and distraction and the divisive element which prevents unity, or any greater good than that which binds it together and makes it one? There is unity where there is community of pleasures and pains—where, as far as may be, all the citizens are glad or grieved alike over the same births and the same deaths. Individuality in these feelings is a dissolving force—when one part of the citizens are stricken with grief and the other transported with joy over the same experiences of the city or its inhabitants. Such differences usually rise from disagreement in the state over the use of such words as 'mine' and 'not mine', 'another's' and 'not another's', and the best ordered state is the one in which the greatest number of people apply the terms 'mine' and 'not mine' in the same way to the same thing. And so the best state is that which bears the closest resemblance to the individual human being. To take the human body as our example—when anyone hurts his finger, the whole fellowship of body and soul which is bound into a single organisation, namely, that of the ruling power within it, feels

the hurt, and is all in pain at once, whole and hurt part together. And so we say that the man has a pain in his finger;
and the same account may be given about any other part of
the body which feels a sensation of pain at suffering or of
pleasure at the alleviation of suffering.

Yes, he said. And I agree with you that in the best ordered
state there is the nearest approach to this common feeling
which you describe.

Then when any one of the citizens experiences anything
good or bad, the whole state will make his case their own and
will share his joy or his sorrow?

Yes, he said. That must certainly be so in a well ordered
state. . . .

Our citizens will have a common interest; each will call
that interest 'mine'; so they will share each other's pleasures
and pains. And the reason for this, beyond the general arrangements of the state, will be that the guardians will have wives
and children in common. And this unity of feeling we admitted
to be the greatest good—as was implied in our comparison of a
well ordered state to the relation of the body and the limbs
when affected by pleasure or pain. Thus, the community of
wives and children among the protectors is clearly the cause
of the greatest good to the state. This is consistent with the
other principles we were affirming, for we said, did we not,
that if the governing class were to govern in reality they must
not have houses or land or any other possession of their own,
but must receive what they need for their sustenance from the
other citizens as wages for their guardianship and lay it out in
common? Community of property and of families will tend to
make them more truly guardians and prevent the disruption
of the city which would arise if everyone differed about
'mine' and 'not mine'; if each man dragged off any acquisition he made into a separate house of his own; if each man had
a separate wife and children of his own, and thus implanted in
the city the individual pleasures and griefs of individuals.
Rather they will possess one single belief about what is their
own and be all concerned in the same purpose, and so will all
be, so far as is possible, simultaneously affected by pleasure

and pain. And if their own persons are their only private property and everything else is common, lawsuits and prosecutions will almost have disappeared among them; they will be free from all those quarrels that arise among men over money, children or relatives. And since the governing classes will never be at odds amongst themselves there will be no danger that the rest of the city will be divided either against them or against one another. I am almost ashamed to go on and mention the petty meannesses which they will escape—such as, for example, the flattery of the rich by the poor, and all the perplexities and worries of bringing up children and of finding money for the support of their households; the borrowing and repudiation, the scraping together of money to give to their wives and servants to manage for them. The nature and extent of men's sufferings in this way are obvious, ignoble too, and not worth mention. They will be rid of all those troubles, and their life will be more blessed than the blissful life of Olympian victors. For the victory they win is the salvation of the whole city, and sustenance and all that life requires is the crown given to them and their children. Their own city gives them privileges in their lifetime, and a fitting burial after their death.

(Plato, *Republic* 462a–e; 464b–465e)

ARISTOTLE ON COMMUNISM

Plato and Aristotle both saw the goal of politics as human good (see p. 44). Perhaps today we lack a clear view on this matter? Plato and Aristotle further held that political aims had to be realised by human means in the form of trained characters. Is it not true, however, to say that the sheer size of the modern state, the influence of scientific conceptions and the analogies of technology make us think that salvation lies rather in economic schemes and planning, industrial techniques and 'social engineering'? Do we not put too much trust in the institutional, manipulative approach? In his hopes for character-training of his citizens Plato was an idealist; Aristotle took a more common-sense view; as we see from his rejection of Plato's proposed communism:

Let us next consider what our arrangements about property should be—should the citizens of the perfect state hold their property in common or not? This matter may be discussed separately from the enactments concerning women and children. Even if the women and children belong to individuals, in accordance with the custom which is now universal, may there not be an advantage in having and using possessions in common? The following three approaches are possible: (1) the farms may be separate property, but the produce may be put into the common stock for consumption (as is the practice of some non-Greek races). Or (2) the land may be common and farmed in common, but the produce divided amongst individuals for their private use; this is a form of common property which is said to exist among certain barbarians. Or (3) the land and the produce may alike be common.

When the tillers of the soil are not the owners, the situation will be different and easier to handle; but when they till the ground for themselves the regulations for common ownership will give more causes for discontent. If they do not share equally in enjoyment and the work of production, those who toil greatly but receive little will naturally complain about those who toil little and receive or consume much. And in general to live together and share all our human affairs is always difficult, but especially to share property. This is illustrated by the partnerships of fellow-travellers, for almost the greatest number of them quarrel over everyday matters and dispute over trifles. It is so with servants; we are most likely to take offence at those whom we employ most often for ordinary attendance upon us.

These are only a few of the disadvantages which community of property brings with it; the present system, if improved as it might be by good morals and by the regulation of correct legislation, would be greatly superior, and would have the merits of both arrangements. Property in a certain sense should be common, but, as a general rule, private. For when every person has a distinct interest there will be no cause for mutual complaints and there will be greater progress, because everyone will be attending to his own business; while on the other hand virtue will be exercised to make 'friends' goods common goods', as the proverb has it. Such a system exists even now in outline in some states, showing that it is not impracticable, but, in well ordered states, exists already to a certain extent and may be carried further. For although the individual has his own property, some things he will put at the service of his friends, and of others he shares the use with them. In Sparta, for instance, people use one another's slaves as virtually their own, as well as horses and hounds; and they also use the produce in the fields if, while on a journey, they need supplies. It is clearly better that property should be private, but the use of it common. And to make people well disposed to one another in this way is the special task of the legislator. Further, to feel that a thing is one's own piece of property makes an inexpressibly great difference to the pleasure felt; for the universal feeling of love for oneself is an instinct implanted by nature and not given for no purpose. But selfishness is rightly censured; for this is not merely to love oneself but to do so in excess, just as covetousness means loving money more than one ought; for all, or nearly all, men love money and other such things in some degree. Again, there is the greatest pleasure in bestowing favours and assistance on friends or visitors or companions, which can only be rendered when a person has private property. These advantages do not come to those who carry the unification of the state too far. Besides, the practice of two virtues is manifestly destroyed: first, temperance towards women (for it is an honourable action to abstain from another's wife for the sake of temperance); second, liberality in relation to possessions (for when all things are held in common, no one will any longer be able to set an example of liberality or perform a single liberal action, since liberality consists in the use which is made of possessions).

Such legislation may have an attractive appearance of benevolence; for people who are told about it welcome it gladly, imagining that it will result in a marvellous friendliness of everyone towards everyone else, especially when somebody is heard denouncing the evils at present existing in states (lawsuits about contracts, trials for perjury, flattery of the rich, and so on) as being due to the fact that property is not owned in common. But the real cause of these evils is not the absence of communism, but the wickedness of human nature. In fact, we see far more quarrels occurring among those who own or use property in common than among those who have their property separate—though there are not many of the former in comparison with the large numbers who have private property.

Again, it is just to state not only all the evils from which men will be saved by the adoption of communism but also all the good things which they will lose. The life which one could lead under this system seems utterly impracticable. The cause of Socrates' error (in Plato's *Republic*) must be assigned to the false conception of unity with which he begins. Unity there ought to be, both of the family and of the state, but only in certain ways. For a state may attain such a degree of unity as to be no longer a state, or it may reach such a stage of unification that, without in fact ceasing to exist, it will become an inferior state, just like a harmony turning into unison or rhythm into a single foot. The proper thing is for the state, while being a multitude, to be made a partnership and a unity by means of education, as has been said before; and it is strange that the author of a system of education which he thinks will make the state morally good should fancy that he can improve society by measures of this sort instead of by manners and culture and laws, like those which prevail at Sparta and Crete respecting common messes, whereby the legislator made property common. And this very point also must not be overlooked—that we must pay attention to the length of time and the long period of years in which it would have been noticed if these measures were good; for almost everything has been found out, though sometimes no work of synthesis has been done, and in other cases men do not make use of the knowledge which they have.

(Aristotle, *Politics* 1262^{b}37–1264^{a}3)

For Aristotle's emphasis on the idea of partnership (expressed in the last paragraph above) and Plato's tendency to think in terms of the community and its happiness as seen in the two *Republic* passages on pp. 80 ff., see p. 14.

THE RIGHT REGULATION OF PROPERTY

In this excerpt Aristotle continues his reflections on ownership. Would you agree with the dictum of a modern political scientist that 'liberty is a function of private property'?

Some people think that the right regulation of property is the main point of all, for that is the question upon which all revolutions turn. Phaleas of Chalcedon,[1] recognising this fact, was the first to suggest as an expedient measure that the citizens of a state ought to have equal possessions. He thought that in a new colony it would be easy to secure equalisation, but when a state was already established it could not take place so easily; and that then the simplest way of attaining the desired objective would be for the rich to give and not receive marriage dowries, and for the poor not to give but to receive them.

In the *Laws*[2] Plato thought that up to a certain point inequality ought to be allowed, forbidding, as has already been observed, any citizen to acquire more land than would make his estate five times the size of the smallest. But those who make such laws should remember what they tend to forget—that when fixing the amount of property legislators ought also to regulate the number of children; for if the children are too many in number for the property, the law is quite sure to be broken; and apart from the violation of the law, it is a bad thing that many from being rich should become poor. For it is hard for such men not to stir up revolutions in the state. That the equalisation of property has its effects on the community of the citizens to an important degree was clearly recognised even by some of the old legislators. Solon and others made laws to prohibit any individual from possessing as much land as he desired; and there are other laws in states which prohibit the sale of property; among the Locrians, for instance, there is a law which lays down that a man must not sell his property unless he can prove that manifest misfortune has befallen him.

[1] Of Phaleas the egalitarian we know no more than is stated here.
[2] The *Laws*, which occupied Plato's last years, give his revised views on statesmanship.

Again, there have been laws which order the preservation of the old allotments. The repeal of this restriction on the island of Leucas made the Leucadian constitution unduly democratic, for those filling the various offices no longer had the prescribed property-qualifications. Yet, where equality of property is maintained, the amount may be either too large and encourage luxury, or too small and create a penurious standard of living. The legislator, therefore, ought clearly not only to aim at equalisation of estates but also at securing a moderate size. In addition, even if a moderate property for all were prescribed, he would be no nearer his objective, for it is not men's possessions but their desires which require to be equalized—which is impossible unless there is an adequate system of education provided by the laws. But perhaps Phaleas would reply that this is just what he intends; and that, in his opinion, there ought to be in states not only equal property but equal education as well. But the nature of the education needs to be defined; there is no use in having one and the same for all if it is of the kind that makes men avaricious or ambitious for status, or both. For civil strife is caused not only by inequality of property but also by inequality of honours, though the two motives work in opposite ways; the common people quarrel about the inequality of property, the upper class if honours are equally distributed, bringing it about that (as the poet says)

'Noble and base in equal honour stand'.

There are crimes to which men are impelled by need, for which Phaleas thinks that the equalisation of property would be a cure—preventing highway robbery by taking away the motive of cold or hunger. But men also do wrong to gain pleasure and to satisfy desire; they wish to cure some desire which goes beyond the bare necessities of existence and which preys upon them. But this is not the only reason; they may desire to enjoy the pleasures that are not accompanied by pain, and so commit crimes.

What remedy is there, then, for these three classes of offenders? For the first, moderate possessions and occupation; for the second, habits of temperance. As for the third kind, any people who desire pleasures which depend on themselves will find no cure for their desires except the one derived from philosophy, for the other pleasures require the help of our fellow-creatures. The truth is that the greatest crimes are occasioned by excess and not by necessity. Men do not become tyrants in order to avoid shivering with cold; and so high honours are accorded to one who kills a tyrant, but not to one who kills a thief. And thus we see that the institutions put forward by Phaleas are efficacious only against petty crimes.

But they are open to a further objection. Phaleas' ideas are principally designed to promote the internal welfare of the state. But the legislator should also have regard to its relations with neighbouring peoples and to all who are outside of it. It is essential that the constitution be framed with a view to military strength, about which Phaleas has said nothing. And the same applies to property: there should be not only enough to meet the requirements of the state internally, but also to meet the dangers which come from outside. Hence the state should possess neither so great an amount of wealth that more powerful neighbours may be tempted by it, while its owners are unable to repel their attackers; nor yet so small an amount that the state cannot sustain a war even against equal and similar states. Phaleas has laid down no rule; but we should recall that abundance of wealth is an advantage. Perhaps therefore the best limit to prescribe is that it must not profit a more powerful neighbour to make war upon the state because of its excessive wealth, but only just as it might do even if the citizens did not possess so much property. For example, when Autophradates was about to lay siege to Atarneus, its ruler Eubulus asked him to consider how long it would take him to complete the capture of the city, and then to reckon up the cost of a war of that duration. 'For,' he added, 'I am willing for a smaller sum than that to abandon Atarneus now.' These words of Eubulus caused Autophradates to think again and to give up the siege.

There is, then, some value for sure in equality of wealth as a safeguard against civil quarrels, but we must not exaggerate its efficacy, which is not very great. The nobles will be dissatisfied because they think that they are worthy of more than an equal share of honours;—this is often found to be a cause of revolutionary conspiracy amongst the upper class. Also, the avarice of human beings is insatiable. At first a dole of a mere two obols is enough; then, when that has become established as the due payment, they go on asking for more until their demands become unlimited; for appetite is in its nature unlimited, and most men live only for the satisfaction of it. The starting-point of reform lies not so much in levelling estates as in training the nobler kind of natures not to wish for excessive wealth and in preventing the baser sort from getting more— which means they should be weaker but not downtrodden.

(Aristotle, *Politics* 1266ᵃ37–1267ᵇ9)

SENECA ON RICHES

Officially, Stoicism regarded wealth as something indifferent in the pursuit of virtue—its presence or absence made no difference to the committed Stoic's zeal for the quest. The Younger Seneca (see p. 21 f.), himself a very wealthy man, took an independent line, holding that to refuse riches entry into one's home is a confession that one does not know how to use them properly; wealth, in fact, enables the philosopher to put his theories into practice—an argument which modern socialist millionaires would recognise and respect. Compare Aristotle's argument on wealth as a means to the exercise of the virtue of liberality, p. 84. How convincing a case does Seneca advance?

And so, if any of those who bark against philosophy should ask the usual question: 'Why, then, do you talk so much more bravely than you live? Why do you speak with humility in the presence of a superior and consider money a necessary part of your equipment, and why are you stirred by a loss? Why do your dinners not conform to your own teaching? Why is your furniture so elegant? Why is the wine drunk at your table older than you yourself? Why the ostentatious aviary? Why are trees planted on your estate which will supply nothing but shade? Why does your wife wear in her ears jewellery whose price equals the revenue of a rich house? Why are your young slaves dressed in expensive clothes? Why is it a special art to wait at your table? Why is the plate not set out carelessly and casually, and why is the service carried out with such expertise? Why is there a professional in charge of the carving of the meat?' Add too if you like this: 'Why do you have possessions across the seas? Why do you own more than you have actually seen? It's a shameful business—you are either so careless that you do not know your handful of slaves by sight, or so pampered that you own more than your memory can take account of!' Later I shall surpass your reproaches and find more fault with myself than you can imagine; in the meanwhile this is my reply: 'I am not a wise man in the sense of the Stoic ideal—nor, to feed your malevolence, shall I ever be. And so do not demand that I should be equal to the best, but that I should be better than the wicked. It is enough for me if each day I cut down the number of my vices and blame my mistakes. I have not yet attained to perfect health, nor in fact shall I attain to it. The same charge has been levelled against Plato, Epicurus and Zeno; they did not profess to say how they lived, but only how they ought to live.'

Not one penny will a wise man admit over his threshold that makes a dishonest entry; but he will not repulse or exclude great wealth that is the gift of Fortune and the fruit of virtue. Why should he grudge it good quarters? Let it come, let it be warmly received. But he will not flaunt it, nor will he hide it—the one action is that of a foolish mind, the other of a timid and petty mind which makes him keep in his pocket a great blessing, as it were—nor will he, as I have said, expel it from his house. For what will he say to it? Will it be, 'You are of no use to me,' or 'I do not know how to use riches'? In the same way that he will prefer, even if he is able to accomplish a journey on foot, to climb into a carriage, so he will prefer, even if he is able to be poor, to be rich. And so he will possess wealth, but on the understanding that it is fickle and likely to take to flight, and he will not allow it to be a burden either to himself or to anyone else. He will give of it—why have you pricked up your ears? why do you get your pocket ready?—he will give of it either to good men or to those whom he will be able to make good men; choosing the most worthy after the deepest deliberation, he will give of his wealth as one who remembers that he must give account as much of his expenditure as of his receipts; he will give of it only for a just and defensible reason, for wrong giving must be considered a shameful waste; he will have his pocket accessible, but it will have no hole in it—a pocket from which much can come forth but nothing fall.

(Seneca, *De Vita Beata* 17.1–18.2; 23.3–5)

(*The value of money for doing good must not be under-rated, even though its possession may lay us open to particular temptations. Seneca here indicates the principle, ' To do a great good do a little evil'.*)

'What then?' you say, 'will the wise man not approach with a bribe a door which is guarded by a surly keeper?' Of course he will; if some necessary business summons him he will make the venture and will placate the keeper, whatever his manner, as one pacifies a dog with a dainty; and he will not think it improper to pay something in order to pass over the threshold, reflecting that even on some bridges one cannot cross without payment of toll.

(Seneca, *De Constantia Sapientis* 14.2)

IV. The Individual and the State: Tensions[1]

DIVINE AND HUMAN LAW

The theme of Sophocles' tragedy *Antigone* (probably produced in 441 B.C.) is conflict—between Creon, ruler of Thebes, who represents law and order, and Antigone who upholds the unwritten divine dispensation (for which idea, strongly emphasised later by the Stoics, see the passage from Cicero, *De Re Publica* 3.22, p. 78). After Oedipus' death his two sons Eteocles and Polynices fought for the mastership of the city, killing each other in the final encounter of the siege. Creon, now firmly established in power, decreed a splendid funeral for Eteocles, the defender of Thebes, while for the body of Polynices he ordered the supreme indignity that it should be left where it was, unburied—something peculiarly horrible in the eyes of Greeks. Though the death penalty had been promulgated for anyone who disobeyed this order, Antigone, sister of the two brothers, buried the corpse, moved by her deep sense of what is right, and so went to her own death (by suicide).

Antigone and her sister Ismene (cp. the reference towards the end of the passage to putting 'them both' to death), as the nearest kin to the dead, are under a sacred obligation towards them, though Ismene in fact refuses to go so far in the matter as Antigone. In the play the major issues of liberty, obedience and conscience are raised. The extract chosen is part of a discussion between Creon and his son Haemon, to whom Antigone is betrothed. The element of debate is an important one in Greek tragedy; because of the work of many of the Sophists, the rhetorical mode predominated in the educational system and cultural atmosphere of fifth-century Athens.

Jean Anouilh (b. 1910), the French dramatist, has written a modern version of the story (1949). How far are law, religion and morality to be distinguished, and legal rights and duties correlative?

---

[1] In this chapter we shall look at some situations in which there is a clash between public policy and private interest, conscience or inclination.

Creon: He who is a righteous master of his house will also be a righteous statesman. To offend against the laws by violence or to presume to give orders where in fact one should obey is wrong, and I will have none of it. He whom the state appoints must be obeyed in small matters and in great, in just and unjust commandments. The obedient man, I should be confident to affirm, would govern well, and would cheerfully be governed, and would remain a true and loyal comrade, firm in the ranks amid the storm of war. There is no greater curse than anarchy. It ruins states, lays homes low, breaks up in rout allied troops. But discipline saves the lives of many honest folk. We must therefore assist the cause of order, and this means we must make no concession at all to a woman's will. Better to be beaten, if need be, by a man, than let a woman get the better of us.

Chorus: Unless old age has robbed me of my wits, I think the tenor of your words is sound.

Haemon: Father, the gods plant reason in mankind, and of all good gifts it is the highest. I neither am nor would I wish to be clever enough to disprove what you say. Still, another's thought might be useful; and it is my duty, since I am your son, to act as your watchdog, to know what others say and do, and what they find to praise and what to blame. Your frown is enough to silence any word that might offend you. But *I* secretly can gather how acutely the city pities this poor girl doomed to the cruellest and most unjust death that was ever suffered by a woman for a most honourable action—burying a brother killed in battle, rather than leave him naked to be the prey of carrion hounds or birds. Has she not instead earned a gold crown?—such is the secret talk among the citizens.

Father, there is nothing I can value more than your happiness and welfare. What more glorious ornament is there for children than a prospering father's fair fame; or for father than son's? Do not, then, let your first thought be your only thought. Consider if there cannot be some other way. For all those who believe that they alone are wise, that theirs is the only word, the only will, are seen to be empty when opened out for inspection. It is no weakness for a man, though he is wise, to learn when he is wrong and to know when to yield. You see how on the edge of a flooded river trees which bend to the torrent save their shoots, while those that strain against it are destroyed, roots and all. A sailor, too, who keeps the main sheet taut and will not slacken it, eventually goes cruising on a capsized vessel.

And so, pause, and be willing to relent. I think (for what the opinion of a young man is worth) that, while it is an excellent thing to be full of wisdom, since this is rarely found, the next best thing is to listen to advice from the wise.

Chorus: There is some merit in his point of view, and in yours as well, my lord; there is much to be said on both sides.

Creon: Is there indeed? Am I at my time of life to take lessons from a boy like this?

Haemon: No lesson that's dishonest. It is not a matter of age, but of right and wrong.

Creon: Do you consider it right to respect the disobedient?

Haemon: Not if the action also were unprincipled.

Creon: Was this woman not infected by some such taint?

Haemon: The citizens of Thebes think not.

Creon: Are the citizens of Thebes going to give me my orders?

Haemon: Isn't that a rather childish thing to say?

Creon: Am I the ruler of this city or am I not?

Haemon: What sort of state is a one-man state?

Creon: But doesn't every state belong to its ruler?

Haemon: You'd be a fine king—on a desert island.

Creon: This fellow seems to be taking the woman's side.

Haemon: No—unless you be the woman;—then it's your interests I have at heart.

Creon: What, you villain, when everything you say goes against me, your father?

Haemon: Because I see you doing real wrong.

Creon: Wrong? To respect my own authority?

Haemon: Respect? But what you're doing is to trample on all that's holy.

Creon: You're despicable, with no more will than a woman.

Haemon: You will not find me serving what is vile.

Creon: Yet all you say is on her behalf.

Haemon: No, on yours, and mine, and that of the gods of the dead.

Creon: You'll never marry her this side of the grave.

Haemon: Well, if she dies she will not die alone.

Creon: Are you making a threat, you impudent creature?

Haemon: Is it a threat to try to argue against wrong-headed views?

Creon: You'll be sorry, you wrong-headed boy, for arguing thus with me.

Haemon: If you weren't my father I'd have called you mad.

Creon: Don't toady me, you woman's slave.

Haemon: Do you expect to speak and not be answered?

Creon: I do. And what is more, by all the gods above, you'll pay dearly for your insolence to me. Bring out the wretched woman and let her die at once here, with her bridegroom beside her looking on.

Haemon: Not with me looking on, I do assure you; not by my side will she die. Nor from this time shall you see me again. I leave you to act out your madness in the company of those who are willing to witness it.

Chorus: He has gone, my lord, in headlong passion. When a young man like that is angry dire results must follow.

Creon: Let him do or imagine more than a mortal man may; he shall not save those girls from their doom.

Chorus: You mean, then, to put them both to death?

Creon: No, not the one who did not touch the corpse; you were right to say what you did.

Chorus: And by what death do you plan to kill the other?

Creon: She will be taken to some desert place where no one has ever come, and there walled up, alive, within a cave, with a sufficient supply of food to keep us clear of the blood-guiltiness which would otherwise lie upon the state. There she will pray to Death, the god she honours, asking for release from death; or will at last recognise it is lost labour to revere the dead.

(Sophocles, *Antigone* 661–780)

EURIPIDES AND THE IDEAL CITY

Euripides' play *The Suppliant Women* (produced about 420 B.C.) is a study in his ideal city, and it too concerns burial rights. The unhappy story of Thebes and the curse upon its ruling house which was a major source of material for the Greek dramatists again forms the background. The mothers of the Seven Heroes who assisted Polynices in his abortive attempt on the city have sought sanctuary at Eleusis, and Theseus, ruler of Athens, takes up their cause at the instance of his mother Aethra. He defeats the Thebans and brings back the bodies of the slain chiefs for proper burial. Not to obtain burial was accounted a calamity worse than death itself. Theseus in the play represents the perfect leader under whom all enjoy full rights and liberty. Set in a heroic age, it has a matching tone of high and chivalrous nobility, exemplified by Aethra's words to her son:

My son, I tell you to look to this first, so that you do not err, despising their appeal to heaven. In this alone you are mistaken, being wise in all else.

And further,—I should have endured in silence if you had not been bound to champion the cause of the oppressed. But as it is, this is the foundation of your fame, and so I am not afraid to exhort you, son, to lay a strong constraining hand upon men of violence who refuse the dead the dues of burial and funeral rites, and stop those people who would subvert the traditional usages of all Greece; for the uniting bond in all states is this— proper respect for law and custom in each citizen.

But some will say that, lacking the power of courageous action, you flinched through fear and lost the chance to win for Athens a crown of glory when you had the chance.

(Euripides, *Supplices* 301–315)

Later there is a debate between a herald from Thebes and Theseus about monarchy and democracy and the rights of citizens under each. Paradoxically, Theseus, though king of Athens, is shown as founder and upholder of the democratic system in the city, and there is actually evidence that Athenian legend did connect Theseus with the origins of democracy there. In the figure of Theseus, too, the audience were perhaps meant to recall Pericles (who had died in 429 B.C.; see p. 11), and his high ideals.

Herald: Who is the despot of this land? To whom must I proclaim the words of Creon, lord of Thebes since Eteocles was killed at the hands of Polynices at the sevenfold gates?
Theseus: First, stranger, you began your speech on a false note,

looking for a despot here. Our city is ruled not by one man only—Athens is free. Her people in succession rule year by year; no advantage is bestowed on the rich, and the poor have an equal position.

Herald: If we were playing draughts I should have in this an advantage over you: the city from which I come is ruled by one man and not by any mob. There is no one there who makes the people vain and arrogant with his words and twists them this way and that for his own gain; who courts popularity now and greatly humours them, but presently does them harm and then cloaks his faults by laying the blame upon others and thus slips through the net of justice.

How could the people who cannot think straight keep the city on a straight course? Time is a better teacher than haste. But the poor peasant in his plot of ground, even if he were to be rid of ignorance, could not because of his work be expected to have an eye for the well-being of the whole community. This in the wise man's sight is disastrous, when a worthless man, a mere nobody, woos the people and gets himself a name.[1]

Theseus: An eloquent herald this, a trifling babbler! But since you have plunged into this strife, hear what I have to say; you flung down the challenge to an argument.

The state has no worse enemy than the despot, under whom, first, there can be no common laws, but one man rules, keeping in his own hands the law—which means the end of equality. But when the laws are written, then the weak and the wealthy possess equal rights. And yes, the weaker may fling back in the teeth of the prosperous the scoff, if he is insulted. Armed with right the less overcomes the great. Freedom speaks thus:[2] 'What man wishes to bring good counsel for the state before the people?' The man who is ready to respond gains distinction; the one who is not remains silent. Can equality go further?

Besides, when the people steer the country's course, it has a supply to hand of young native champions. But a king regards

[1] Euripides refers to the influence of sophistic rhetoric prevalent in his day.
[2] He quotes the opening formula proclaimed by the herald at the Athenian popular assembly.

this as hateful, and he kills the best men in whom he discerns intellect because he is afraid they will take away his power. How, then, could a state be strong when someone lops off like flower-blooms courageous young spirits as though he were plying his scythe in a meadow in spring? What is the point of gaining wealth and substance for one's children, when all one's toil is only increasing a despot's substance? Or of rearing daughters virtuously at home just to provide a despot with sweet dainties when the fancy takes him, and the parents with a cause for tears? I should rather die than see my daughters ravished.

This is the shaft I launch in reply to yours. But why have you come and what do you want from this land of ours? If you had not been sent as an official messenger from your city, you would have been sorry you had come with all your insolent talk.

(Euripides, *Supplices* 399–459)

The wider context of Euripides' play is a conflict over the human right to decent burial, but in the excerpt just given something of the question of civic rights in relation to the problem of political power is expressed. For monarchy and democracy see the Herodotus passage on p. 27 ff. Our own age is much exercised by the question of rights. How do we make our answer to the following: '"Natural rights" is just simple nonsense' (Bentham); 'Society has this good at least, that it lessens our conceit by teaching us our insignificance' (Thackeray); 'Freedom is a new religion, the religion of our age' (Heine, died 1856)?

RIGHTS AND PROTEST

As at Athens when Solon was empowered to bring in reform (see p. 10), so in early Rome the law of debt was very strict and imprisonment of debtors common. The plebeians were kept in subjection by the patricians (see p. 18). At last resentment gave way to action and (traditionally) in 494 B.C. the plebeians removed themselves in a body from Rome and, having taken up a position on a hill a few miles away, declared that they would found there a new plebeian city. Five such 'secessions of the *plebs*' are recorded between 494 and 287 B.C. Their historicity has often been doubted, but scholarly scepticism has been excessive, and the tradition is probably right concerning a 494

B.C. secession and the foundation then of the tribunate under which the plebeians (or 'commons') were allowed to have, at first two, later four, officers (*tribuni plebis*) to look after their interests. These watch-dogs of the *plebs* were invested with considerable powers, and the tribunate was destined to be an important factor in Roman politics.

The story of the popular secessions, apart from any narrow histori-cal considerations, possesses a particular, symbolic meaning in the development of Rome. Both patricians and plebeians were attached to Rome and its institutions, and throughout their protracted struggle they showed great moderation; rarely was blood actually shed, and there never was civil war. And often when external foes pressed hard they readily laid aside their quarrel to make common cause against the aggressors. The secessions are not represented as 'general strikes' but as acts of separation, unaccompanied by violence, to express protest. They sum up in themselves the mutual attitudes of the two sides and the tenor of their disputes.

In reading the account given by Livy (for whom see p. 21) of the first secession of the *plebs*, we must consider the place and function of popular protest in society; what are its permissible limits to be?

The Menenius Agrippa episode is mythical; the fable Menenius tells on the body and the limbs is to be found elsewhere in ancient literature—see especially St Paul, 1 Corinthians xii, 12–27.

After the consul Vetusius had returned to Rome the first matter which Valerius brought before the Senate was the case of the common people (who had played a great part in winning victory in the recent wars). He proposed that the Senate should declare its policy concerning those who were bound over for debt. When this motion had been rejected Valerius replied: 'I urge domestic harmony, but it does not appeal to you. Mark my words, however: the day will soon come when you will be longing for men of my outlook to advocate the people's cause. So far as I am concerned, I shall not go on frustrating my fellow citizens' hopes and continue to act as Dictator to no purpose.[1] Internal struggles and foreign war made this office of Dictator necessary to the state; peace has been secured

---

[1] In the Roman constitution a *dictator* ('the man who says what is to be done') was a chief magistrate with unlimited power appointed in great emergencies for a limited time and taking precedence over all other magis-trates. Julius Caesar had absolute power as *dictator* from 48 B.C. till his assas-sination four years later (see p. 19).

abroad, but here at home there are obstacles in the way to it.
I would rather face the trouble when it breaks out as a private
citizen than as Dictator.' So saying he left the Senate-house
and resigned his office. It was clear to the people that the cause
of his resignation was resentment at the unjust treatment meted
out to them. He had been unable to keep his promise to bring
relief to them, but this at least was through no fault of his, and
so with marks of favour and approval they attended him as he
retired to his house.

The senators now began to be alarmed, fearing that if the
army should be disbanded leaders of the people would again
hold secret meetings and seditious gatherings. The troops had
in fact been raised by order of the Dictator, yet because they
had taken the military oath to obey the consuls as their com-
manders they could still be regarded as bound by it; on this
assumption, then, and on the pretext that the Aequians had
recommenced hostilities, the senators ordered the army to
march. This speedily brought the matter to a head. At first, we
are told, there was talk amongst the soldiers of killing the
consuls so that they could thus be freed from their oath of
allegiance; but when they had been warned that they could
not be absolved from a sacred obligation by a crime, they
followed the advice of a man called Sicinius and without
orders from the consuls withdrew to the Sacred Mount, which
is situated across the river Anio, three miles from Rome. . . .
There, without any leader, they fortified their camp with
stockade and trench, and continued quietly, taking only what
they needed for subsistence, for a number of days. They neither
received any provocation nor gave any.

In Rome there was a great panic, and all activity came to a
halt through the apprehension felt by both sides. The common
people, abandoned as they were by their friends in the army,
were afraid of violence at the hands of the senators, who were
afraid, in their turn, of the commons left behind in Rome,
being uncertain whether they wished them to go or remain.
Besides, how long would the seceding multitude continue
peaceable? What would happen next should some foreign war
break out in the meanwhile? Clearly the only hope lay in
achieving a solution of the discord between patricians and

plebeians in the state; harmony had to be restored to the country by fair means or foul. The senatorial side accordingly resolved to send as their ambassador to the commons on the Sacred Mount Menenius Agrippa, an eloquent man and liked by the commons as he was one of themselves. Having been admitted to the camp he is reported merely to have related the following parable in the quaint and uncouth style of that age: 'Long ago, when the limbs of the human body did not all agree amongst themselves as they do now, but had each its own thoughts and a voice of its own, the other parts thought it unfair that they should have the worry and trouble of providing everything for the belly, while the belly remained idle in their midst with nothing to do but enjoy the pleasant things they gave it. The discontented limbs therefore conspired together that the hand should carry no food to the mouth, that the mouth should take nothing that was offered to it, and that the teeth should accept nothing to chew. But while they sought in this resentful spirit to starve the belly into submission, they themselves and the whole body wasted away to nothing. From this it was apparent that even the belly has no mean service to perform and that it is not merely a question of its being nourished but that it also nourishes in its turn the rest of the body, giving back to all the parts, through all the veins equally, the blood produced by the process of digestion—the blood on which we depend for our life and vigour.'

Drawing a parallel from this fable to explain the likeness between the internal quarrel of the limbs of the body and the anger of the common people against the Fathers, he succeeded in winning over his hearers. A movement was set on foot to establish harmony and a compromise was reached on these terms: the commons were to have special magistrates of their own to represent them; these officers—'tribunes of the people' —were to be inviolable in their persons and thus above the law, and their function was to protect the common people against the consuls. No man belonging to the senatorial class was to be permitted to hold the office. And so two 'tribunes of the people' were created, Gaius Licinius and Lucius Albinus.

(Livy, *History* 2. 32.8–33.2)

SOCRATES IN PRISON

We pass now from rights to civic duty: we hear Socrates as presented by Plato upholding in the condemned cell the state's authority to judge and punish him and maintaining that it is his duty to submit. In 399 B.C. he was tried and found guilty of 'corrupting the young men and not worshipping the city's gods'. The sophistic movement was thought by many to be largely responsible for the decline and collapse of Athens, and by many Socrates was associated with the Sophists— hence the prosecution. The whole action was mistaken.

Do you think that Socrates' position is fully tenable? How far is one to accept the state of things without trying to change it? Do you agree with the contention that 'while parties ought to have principles, they ought also to change them, and liberty cannot be safe unless they are ready to change them'?

Socrates: Look at it this way. Imagine that I am about to play truant (or whatever we should call the proceeding) and the laws and the commonwealth come and question me: 'Tell us, Socrates,' they say; 'what do you intend to do? Can you deny that by this act which you are contemplating you intend, so far as you have the power, to destroy us—the laws and the whole state as well? Or do you think that that state can exist and not be turned upside down, in which the decisions reached by the courts have no force but are rendered invalid and annulled by private persons?' What shall we say, Crito, in answer to this question and others of the same kind? There is much that could be said by way of protest, especially if one were a trained speaker, against the invalidation of that law which enacts that the judgments of the court shall be binding. Or shall we say to them, 'Yes, but the state has wronged me and did not judge the case correctly'? Shall we say that, or what?
Crito: What you have just said, by all means, Socrates.
Socrates: What if the laws should say, 'Socrates, is this the agreement you made with us, or did you agree to abide by the verdicts pronounced by the state?' If I were surprised at such language, they would probably say: 'Pay no attention to our language, Socrates, but answer our questions; after all, you are used to the method of question and answer. Come now, what fault do you find with us and the state that makes you try

to destroy us? In the first place, did we not give you life? Was it not through us that your father married your mother and begot you? Now tell us, have you any fault to find with those of us laws that are related to marriage?' 'I find no fault,' I should say. 'Or with those that deal with children's upbringing and education, such as you had yourself? Did those of us who are assigned to these matters not give good directions when we instructed your father to give you a cultural and physical education? 'You did,' I should say. 'Very well, then. Since you have been born and reared and educated, can you deny, in the first place, that you were our child and servant, both you and your ancestors? And if this is so, do you imagine that what is right for us is equally right for you, and that whatever we attempt to do to you it is right for you to retaliate? There was no such equality of right between you and your father or your employer, if you had one, which enabled you to retaliate; you were not allowed to answer back if you were scolded or to hit back if you were struck, or to do many similar things. Do you expect to be allowed so to act against your country and its laws that if we undertake to destroy you, thinking it is right, you on your part will undertake to destroy us laws and your country in return, so far as you can, and will claim to have right on your side in doing this, true devotee of goodness that you are? Are you so wise as to have forgotten that your country is something more precious and more to be revered and is holier and in higher esteem among the gods and among men of understanding than your mother and your father and all your ancestors? Do you not realise that you are even more bound to show respect, obedience and a placatory attitude to her when she is angry than to your father? That if you cannot persuade her you must do whatever she orders and suffer in silence whatever she commands you to suffer? And if she orders you to be flogged or imprisoned or if she leads you to war to be wounded or killed, her will is to be obeyed, and this is right? And you must not give way or retreat or leave your post, but in war and in court and everywhere you must do whatever the state, your country, orders, or must show her by persuasion what is really right, but that violence against parents is a sin, and violence against your country is an even greater sin?'—

What shall we reply to this, Crito? That what the laws say is true, or not?

Crito: Yes, I think so.

Socrates: 'Consider, then, Socrates,' the laws would perhaps continue, 'if we are right in saying that in your present attempt you are setting about doing us an injury. Although we brought you into the world and reared and educated you, and have given you and all your fellow-citizens a share in all the good things at our disposal, we nevertheless proclaim, by the very fact of offering the opportunity, that any Athenian, on reaching manhood and seeing for himself the political organisation of the state and us its laws, may, if he is not satisfied with us, take his goods and go away wherever he likes. And none of us stands in the way or forbids any of you to take his possessions and go away wherever he pleases, if we and the state do not please him, whether it be to an Athenian colony or to a foreign country where he will live as an alien. On the the other hand, if any one of you remains here when he can see how we administer justice and govern the state in other respects, we maintain that by so doing he has in fact entered into an agreement to do what we tell him; and we say that anyone who disobeys commits a threefold offence: first because we are his parents, and secondly because we are his guardians; and thirdly because after agreeing to obey us he is neither obeying us nor persuading us that our commands are unjust; and although we put our orders in the form of proposals and not of savage commands, and we grant him the choice of either persuading us or doing what we say, he is in fact doing neither. These are the charges, Socrates, to which you will be liable if you do what you have in mind; and you will be not the least blameworthy of your fellow-citizens but one of the most culpable.' If I said 'Why do you say that?' they would no doubt come back at me with perfect justice and point out that there are very few people in Athens who have made this agreement with them more emphatically than I have. For they would say, 'Socrates, we have strong evidence that you are satisfied with us and the state. You would not have been so exceptionally unwilling to leave your country to visit other states if you had not been exceptionally devoted to it; you have never left the city to attend a festival or for any other purpose except on military service; you have never travelled abroad as other people do, nor have you had any desire to find out about any other city or constitution, but you were contented with us and our city. You have firmly chosen us, and you undertook to live out your life as a citizen in accordance with our commands; and the greatest sign of your satisfaction with Athens is the fact that you have begotten children in it. Furthermore, even at your trial you might have offered exile as your penalty, if you wished, and might have done with the state's permission what you are now trying to do without it. But while on that occasion you put on airs and said you were not concerned if you had to die, and in fact preferred death to banishment, now you show no respect for your former professions, and no regard for us, the laws, whom you are trying to destroy; and you are doing what the lowest menial would do, since you are trying to run away contrary to the compacts and agreements you made with us, to the effect that you would live in accordance with us. First, then, answer this question: Are we or are we not speaking the truth when we say that you agreed, not in word, but by your deeds, to live your life as a citizen in obedience to us?' What is our reply to be, Crito? Are we not obliged to admit it?

Crito: We are, Socrates.

Socrates: 'It is the case, then,' they would say, 'that you are breaking your compacts and agreements with us, though you were not led into them by compulsion or trickery, and were not forced to make your decision within a limited period; you had seventy years in which you could have gone away, if you were not satisfied with us and if you thought the agreements unfair. You did not choose Sparta or Crete [1]—which are your favourite examples of sound government—or any other Greek or foreign state, but you were absent from this city less than the lame or the blind or other handicapped people. You obviously have a singular attachment to this city and us its laws; for who

[1] Socrates (and Plato and Aristotle after him—see pp. 11 and 16 ff.) admired these Dorian states for their devotion to law and order. They were oligarchies, a fact which provided Socrates' accusers with yet one more charge to brandish at him.

would be pleased with a city apart from its laws? And now, after all this, are you not going to honour your agreement? You will, Socrates, if you take our advice; and you will at least avoid making a laughing-stock of yourself for leaving the city. . . .

'Socrates, be guided by us your guardians. Don't think more either of your children or your life or anything else than you do of what is right, so that you may be justified before the rulers of the world below. For neither you nor any that belong to you will be the better for it or more upright or have a clearer conscience in this life or be happier in the next, if you do as Crito says. As it is, you will leave this place in innocence, a sufferer and not a doer of wrong—a victim, not of the laws but of your fellow-men. But if you leave in that dishonourable way, returning evil for evil, and injury for injury, breaking the compacts and agreements which you have made with us, and wronging those whom you least of all ought to wrong, that is to say, your friends, your country, and us, we shall be angry with you while you live, and our brothers, the laws in the world below, will not receive you graciously, for they will know that you have done your best to destroy us. Listen, then, to us and not to Crito.'

This, my dear Crito, I do assure you, is what I seem to hear them murmuring, like the sound of a flute in the ears of the mystics;[1] and the sound of their arguments re-echoes so loudly within me that I cannot hear the other side. I warn you that, so far as my opinion at the moment goes, it will be a waste of time if you argue to the contrary. But if you think you can gain anything by it, say what you like.

Crito: No, Socrates, I have nothing to say.

Socrates: Then leave it alone, Crito, and let us follow this course, since this is the way that God is leading us.

(Plato, *Crito* 50a–54e, with omissions)

---

[1] The reference is to the frenzied worship of the Asiatic goddess Cybele, in which exciting music played a prominent part; it would continue to sound in the rapt worshipper's ears after the musicians had ceased. The religious tone and implications of the whole context are unmistakable.

PATRIOTISM AND SELF-INTEREST

The character of Alcibiades (*c.* 450–404 B.C.) was composed of jarring elements: real intellectual ability and personal charm were offset by a tendency to freakish and affected behaviour. There was a basic instability in his make-up. Reared by his relative Pericles and wealthy by inheritance, he was very much of a 'man about town'. In 422 B.C. he became one of the leading politicians in Athens, and in 415 B.C. was a principal advocate of the expedition to Sicily which was to end in disaster (413 B.C.) but which he saw as an opportunity for Athenian imperial and commercial expansion. He was appointed joint commander with Nicias and Lamachus.

There was at this period a prevailing tendency in the Athenian democracy, largely dominated as it was by seafaring citizens, towards distant, overseas ventures. Pericles had always advised against such schemes, but the large youthful component then in the population of the city, hungry for excitement and military conquests and glory, required little persuasion that the enterprise was suitable; it presented the appearance of easy accomplishment. And then, too, the brilliant Alcibiades urged it, which for many must have been the crowning commendation—although because he was then himself in low water financially and in bad repute he had also a personal motivation, hoping that a successful venture would restore his own fortune and good name.

The mutilation of the *Hermae* (marble or bronze pillars surmounted by a bust; originally representing the god Hermes only, they later were used for portrait busts or for images of other divinities) in 415 B.C. was a foolish escapade in which Alcibiades was charged with being the ringleader. The case was one of sacrilege. Alcibiades was already in Sicily when recalled to face trial, but he fled and eventually made his way to Sparta, where he acted as the avowed enemy of his own country. He subsequently was reconciled to Athens, returning there in 407 B.C. when he was made commander-in-chief of all the land and sea forces in return for his conspicuous military successes on behalf of the Athenians during the four years since 411 B.C., the year of his official recall from banishment. But it was only for short periods that he could command the Athenians' confidence. For allegedly mishandling a military operation he was superseded in 406 B.C. and withdrew from the city. In 404 B.C. he was murdered in exile in Phrygia through the influence of political enemies at home.

Thucydides (see books 5–8 of the *History*) takes the Athenians to task for their attitude to Alcibiades whom they twice rejected at critical moments in their history when his talents might have helped them greatly. On the other hand, he was a gifted egoist of whose trustworthiness people were probably quite right to be doubtful. His career certainly did not turn out well for Athens.

On his escape to Sparta after the *Hermae* incident Alcibiades gave the valuable advice to the Spartans that they should despatch a general to Syracuse in Sicily and occupy and hold Decelea which was in Attic territory. Below are given extracts from the speech which Thucydides puts into Alcibiades' mouth on that occasion. It was an age in which ideas about justice, temperance, patriotism and other such qualities had been challenged (see p. 12, and pp. 59 ff.). The devotion to the ascetic life of reflection shown by his friend Socrates Alcibiades was able to admire but not emulate. Instead, he gained notoriety for his vanity and ostentation, his debaucheries and his impious cavorting—a man of great failings but even greater abilities.

With amazingly frank cynicism he remarks that he and his family before him had supported and used for their own ends the democratic constitution at Athens, which could not be changed safely while the city was under threat from an external enemy. They were not demagogues, nor did they believe in democracy; they had made their way politically by opposing tyranny. In any conflict between ambitious self-interest and the needs of the state, the state, Alcibiades assumes, should take second place. We must note, too, the outrageous argument, smacking of the contemporary sophistic schools, in which he defines the genuine patriot as 'not the one who refuses to attack his country when unjustly deprived of it, but the one whose longing for it is so great that he tries by every means to regain it' (ch. 92. 4).

In the context of this particular issue, we might consider the following claims: that patriotism is a 'salutary defect inherent in humanity'; that 'diplomacy and chicanery are synonomous'; that 'whatever view we may take of its assertion by the individual, self-interest is the best foreign policy for a nation'; that 'a gentleman is one who is careful not to take out of the common stock more than he puts into it'; that 'we need to have restless, ambitious people to stir things up; periodical political revolutions are necessary to the mental health of a community'.

Thucydides' account is a written-up version of the actual speech. That he troubled to give so much space to Alcibiades' sentiments on that occasion is probably to be explained by his desire to emphasise (yet again) the decline in moral standards and the perversion of language current at the time, a subject in which he shows particular interest in the first half (most notably the third book) of the eight books of his *History*.

I must first of all speak about the prejudice you feel against me, so that your attention to what I have to say on matters of common concern may not be distracted by suspicion of me personally. My ancestors used to be the official representatives of Sparta at Athens, but because of some accusation they gave up the position. Then I myself took it on again, putting my services at your disposal, especially in respect of the disaster you suffered at Pylos. I was well disposed to you throughout, but in making peace with the Athenians you acted through my personal enemies and thus enhanced their position and brought me into disrepute. You have no right, then, to blame me for the harm you suffered when I turned to Mantinea and Argos and for the various other ways in which I opposed you. And if at that time when you were suffering any of you were unreasonably angry with me, you ought now to see the matter in its true light and change your mind. Or if anyone thought the worse of me because I was rather on the side of the people, here also he should recognise that this was not a proper reason for being ill-disposed towards me. We in my family have always been against autocrats—democracy is the name given to that dispensation under which there is complete opposition to the wielding of absolute power. On the basis of that understanding our leadership of the common people of Athens has continued to exist. At the same time, since democracy was the form of government at Athens, it was necessary in most respects to fit in with the prevailing conditions. But in view of the existing political indiscipline we tried to be more reasonable in our approach to affairs. There have been people in the past (just as there are today) who used to try to lead the masses into more corrupt ways. And it is just this kind of people who banished me. But we served the whole state as leaders, acting on the principle that we should all join together in preserving the traditional form of government under which the city was greatest and most free, though the true nature of democracy was of course quite well understood by every man of insight; and the superiority of my own insight would be measured by the amount of abuse I could pour out upon it. But about an institution commonly agreed to be absurd nothing new could be said. And to set about changing this institution did not seem a safe thing when you were waging war against us. . . .

I claim too that none of you should think any the worse of me if, despite my previous reputation for being patriotic, I now march vigorously against my country along with her most bitter enemies, nor do I think that suspicion should be cast on what I say on the ground that I exhibit the zeal of an exile. An exile I certainly am from the villainy of those who banished me, but not from the power of rendering you assistance, if you will heed what I say. But the more dangerous enemies of Athens are not people like you who have done her some hurt in open warfare but those who have forced her friends to join the other side. For me love of country consists not in suffering injustice, as I am doing now, but in the feeling that I once lived in the secure enjoyment of my rights as a citizen. Nor yet do I consider that I am now attacking a city that is still my country; it is rather the case that I am trying to recover one that has ceased to be mine. The true patriot is not the one who refuses to attack his country when unjustly deprived of it, but the one whose longing for it is so great that he tries by every means to regain it. And so, Spartans, I believe that you should not hesitate to make use of my services for facing every kind of danger and hardship, bearing in mind the argument that everyone puts forward and realising that if I did you a great deal of harm when I was your enemy I could as your friend be of considerable benefit to you: I only conjectured your intentions, whereas I know those of the Athenians. My advice to you is to grasp the fact that it is your fundamental interests which are now being discussed; do not flinch from mounting the campaigns against Sicily and Attica; you need take the field in Sicily with only a small part of your forces to ensure great gains and to destroy both the existing power and the future prospects of the Athenians. After that you yourselves will live in safety and be the leaders of the whole of Greece, which will submit to your authority voluntarily, not through force but from goodwill.

                                                   (Thucydides 6. 89, 92)

DUTY AND DESIRE—CONFLICT

The fourth book of the *Aeneid* has aroused more interest than any
other in Virgil's epic poem (see p. 21) because of his sympathetically
tender treatment of romantic love. Dido, queen of Carthage, the only
great heroine created by a Roman poet to have become part of world
literature, falls in love with Aeneas when she gives him and his
wandering Trojans hospitality. Aeneas reciprocates, but eventually
he receives a divine warning to resume his mission—the re-founding
of Troy in a Western land, an elusive goal. The new Troy is of course
Rome, and in the rift that develops between Dido and Aeneas we
have a reminder of the three Punic Wars fought between Carthage and
Rome (264–146 B.C.) which resulted in Rome's victory and domina-
tion of the Mediterranean.

The placing of duty before personal inclination was an ideal
traditionally regarded with great reverence by the Romans (see p. 23),
and this theme is a major one in the *Aeneid*. In the interchange given
here Dido speaks emotionally, Aeneas with measured logic; but for all
that, his involvement is real and deep. He has not deceived Dido, but
she has deceived herself; he speaks with a cold formality simply to
prevent himself from breaking down and yielding. He is subject to a
higher power and must do its bidding, an obedience which is an essential element in his *pietas* (see p. 23): 'It is not of my own free will that
I sail onward towards Italy.' A modern editor writes well on Aeneas'
situation:

> His speech, though we may not like it, was the Roman answer to
> the conflict between two compelling forms of love, an answer such
> as a Roman Brutus once gave, when he executed his two sons for
> treason against Rome. It is no fault of Virgil's that the harsh con-
> flict between duty and desire is what it is; and given that conflict,
> Virgil knew that this was how he must show it. Aeneas has wronged
> Dido, and he knows it; he has wronged God, and he knows it;
> atonement either way means pain for ever; and it is our pity that
> we should give him, not our scorn.[1]

Do we lay too little stress on duty today? Has society relaxed its
standards too much? Which is more effective and beneficial ultimately
—a system of law based on 'command' supported by force, or one
based on 'obligation' supported by reason?

[1] R. G. Austin, *Aeneid* IV (O.U.P., 1963), p. 106.

Aeneas was struck dumb by the sight, he was out of his wits, his hair stood up as he shivered with fear, his voice stuck in his throat. He burned to flee away from the pleasant land and be gone, so awed was he by the peremptory warning from the gods. But what was he to do? How could he dare to approach the infatuated queen and win her round? What would be the best opening words for him to choose? Swiftly he turned it over in his mind, now favouring one plan, now another, and hastily considering the various aspects of the matter and all the possibilities. As he wavered this seemed the better policy: he called Mnestheus and Sergestus and brave Serestus, telling them to get the fleet ready in silence, muster their comrades on the shore and prepare their tackle, but conceal the reason for the change of plan. Meanwhile he would see Dido, for in her ignorance and trusting innocence she would not expect that so great a love could be broken; he would attempt to approach her and look for the best time to talk to her, the right way to solve the problem. His men at once gladly obey his command and carry out his bidding.

But the queen—who could deceive one in love?—sensed in advance the planned deceit. She did not have to be told, but early realised what would happen, full of fear even when as yet everything was safe. As before, cruel Rumour brought word, telling her in her nervous state the news that the fleet was being equipped for sailing. She raged, unable to come to grips with the situation, and she raved all aflame through the entire city, like a Bacchanal stirred to frenzy by the shaken emblems of Bacchus when, hearing the worshippers cry out the god's name, she is fired every second year by the festival revels and at night Mount Cithaeron summons her with its din.[1] At length she accosted Aeneas, speaking first, and used these words:

'Traitor! Did you actually hope that you would be able to cloak so foul a crime and to leave my land without saying a word? Can neither our love keep you, nor the pledge once given, nor the doom of a cruel death for Dido? Are you so unfeeling that you labour at your fleet under a wintry sky, and

[1] A festival in honour of Bacchus, god of wine, was celebrated at Thebes every second year.

hasten to pass over the high seas in the face of northern gales? Why, if you were not in quest of a home in some alien land unknown to you and if ancient Troy itself were still standing, would you have planned to sail even there in your ships over stormy seas? Is it from me that you are trying to escape? By these tears of mine, by your own right hand (for I have left myself, poor soul that I am, no other appeal), by our union, by our wedlock begun—if ever I have been kind to you, if anything about me has appealed to you, have pity for the ruin of a home, and if it is not too late to beg you, please, I ask you, change your mind. It was because of you that I brought down on myself the hatred of the Numidian chiefs and made the Tyrians my enemies; for you, also, I have lost my honour and that former fame by which alone I had any hope of immortality. In whose hands are you leaving me to die—guest, for I cannot call you husband any more and that is all there is left for me to call you? What kind of future do I have now? Do I wait till my brother Pygmalion comes and destroys my walls, or the Gaetulian[1] Iarbas marries me by capture? At least, if I had a child of yours conceived before your flight, if in my hall a tiny Aeneas were playing whose face, in spite of all, would bring back yours to me, I should not think myself so utterly defeated and deserted.'

She finished. He, remembering Jupiter's warning, held his eyes steadfast and with a struggle tried to smother the deep pain within him. At last he replied, briefly: 'Your Majesty, I shall never deny that I am your debtor for the many kindnesses which you can set forth in speech, nor shall I tire of the memory of Elissa[2] so long as I have consciousness and the breath of life controls these limbs. Concerning the facts of the situation I shall say little. I had no thought of veiling my present departure under deceit—do not imagine that. Nor have I ever made any marriage rite my pretext nor entered such a compact. If destiny had allowed me to shape my life according to my own pleasure and deal with my problems at my own will, my first concern would be the city of Troy and the sweet relics of my kinsmen; Priam's high house would still

---

[1] The Gaetulians were an African people, living in what we call Morocco.
[2] Elissa—a name of Dido.

remain and I should have set up with my own hand a restored Pergamus for the vanquished. But in fact Apollo at Grynium where he gives divination in the Lycian oracle has insistently ordered me to lay hold of the great realm of Italy. This is my love, this is my homeland now. If you, Phoenician as you are, are charmed by the towers of Carthage and the sight of this North African city, why should one grudge the Trojans their settling in Italy? [1] It is as right for us as it was for you to seek a kingdom in foreign soil. To me, each time the night casts her dewy shadows over the earth, each time the fiery stars leap up, in a dream my father Anchises' troubled ghost comes in warning, comes to appal; to me comes the thought of young Ascanius [2] and the wrong done to one who is so dear, whom I am defrauding of his Italian kingdom and predestined lands. Now too the messenger of the gods, sent by Jupiter himself—I swear it by your head and my head—has carried his command down through the swift breezes. With my own eyes I saw the divine messenger in the clear light of day entering the city gate and these ears drank in his words. Cease to vex yourself, and me also, with these protests. It is not of my own free will that I sail onwards towards Italy.'

(Virgil, *Aeneid* 4. 279-361)

[1] Dido herself and her followers had founded Carthage after much wandering.

[2] Ascanius, also called Iulus in the *Aeneid*, was Aeneas' son by his wife Creusa who disappeared in the fall of Troy, recounted in *Aeneid* 2.

V. Women and the State

In Greek society women generally had a subordinate position, though this statement is open to not a few qualifications. They were certainly barred from politics, but participation in the governing of the *polis* was considered to be only for those who could help to defend it by wearing armour and carrying weapons. Besides, the Greeks in common with the Romans, Chinese and other peoples, saw society as a collection of families, and it therefore seemed natural that the heads of families should have the direction of society's affairs in their hands.

Evidence is sparse on the subject, but while encouragement for women to develop their personalities in the same way that was open to men was lacking and certain definite restrictions on them were laid down, they nevertheless were not so confined as to be unable to have a social life of some kind; Euripides more than once comments (adversely) on women bringing back items of gossip to the home from visits to friends. And most probably women went to the theatre.

However, whatever the reasons, women in fifth-century Athens did not really enjoy wide freedom of choice and action, though domestic happiness and satisfaction were clearly a possibility for them, as we learn from vase-paintings and funerary inscriptions. On the subject of women the comment that 'history as it is written leaves out half the things that history ought to discuss' seems particularly applicable. What are the criteria we should use to establish the status of women in any society?

THE DARK SIDE

We turn for our first piece of evidence to Euripides, who was notably interested in feminine psychology and showed much sympathy and understanding. Here he gives the dark side of the picture; his formidable heroine Medea (who, having been thrown over by the husband she has so greatly helped, carries out a terrible revenge) is speaking:

We women are the most unhappy breed. First of all we have to buy a husband at an exorbitant price [1]—and acquire a master over our bodies. This is bad enough, but there is worse to come; we run our greatest risk in not knowing whether the husband will turn out good or bad. Divorce gives women a bad name, and we are not even allowed to reject a suitor.[2] Then when she comes to new customs and habits the bride must be a seer to discover what she did not learn at home, how best to manage her mate. If we train ourselves well this way and our husband lives with us having no inclination to plunge against the yoke, our lot is enviable. But otherwise, there is no help for the situation except death. The man, when he is tired of the company at home, goes out and looks for consolation by turning to some friend or kindred spirit. We can look to one heart alone for comfort. Yet we, they tell us, live a life unthreatened by danger at home, while they fight in battle with the spear. Their reasoning is false. I would rather stand under the shield as a combatant three times than undergo childbirth once.

(Euripides, *Medea* 231–251)

WOMEN AND THE ABOLITION OF WAR— POLITICAL AND DIPLOMATIC MOVES

In 411 B.C. Aristophanes (see p. 12) brought out one of his best plays, the *Lysistrata* (which may freely be rendered *Mrs Demobiliser*). The plot is simple but immensely funny with a characteristic vein of seriousness running through it. The women of Greece, being utterly tired of the long war, have decided, under the leadership of an Athenian matron Lysistrata, to form a conspiracy and refuse all sexual contact to the men until they come to their senses and make peace. The women urge a political solution on the basis of negotiation, as we see from the following passage between Lysistrata and a magistrate. The upshot is that, both sides having suffered enough from deprivation, a distressed-looking ambassador arrives from Sparta demanding in broad Doric an interview with the authorities; he is followed soon after by plenipotentiaries and with the aid of Lysistrata a truce is speedily concluded.

[1] A reference to the dowry system in Greece.
[2] The parents chose a daughter's husband.

The notion of women forming conspiracies for public or private ends appealed to Aristophanes as a comic theme, no doubt as being so unlikely in contemporary Athens. The *Thesmophoriazusae* ('Women celebrating the Festival of the Thesmophoria') is a farce constructed on the alleged misogynistic tendencies of the tragedian Euripides (one of Aristophanes' favourite butts), and the *Ecclesiazusae* ('Women in Parliament') is a skit on the communism Plato preaches in the *Republic* (see p. 80 ff.) and on his belief in the equality of the sexes (for which see p. 122 ff.).

Magistrate: How, then, can you settle and resolve these manifold complications that afflict the nations?

Lysistrata: Quite easily.

Magistrate: How? Tell me.

Lysistrata: Just as we take a skein when it is all tangled up and unravel it with our spindles, drawing it this way and that, so we shall disentangle this war if anyone lets us, drawing it this way and that by means of embassies.

Magistrate: Do you expect, you silly creatures, to disentangle a dreadful state of affairs with your wool and threads and spindles?

Lysistrata: Yes, and if there was any sense in you, you would administer all your affairs as though you were dealing with wool.

Magistrate: How? Enlighten me.

Lysistrata: In the first place, you ought, as if washing away the dirt of a fleece in a bath, to have flogged the rascals headlong out of the city and to have picked out the briars; and you ought to have torn in pieces those who combine and band closely together to win various magistracies—and you ought to have plucked their scalps; and then you ought to have carded public good-feeling into a basket of love and unity, mixing up both the whole body of resident-aliens and any stranger or friend in our midst, as well as anyone in debt to the treasury. And then there are the cities, our colonies—we mustn't overlook them; they are our shreds of wool, lying about scattered and uncared for. You ought to have gathered the wool from all these, bringing it into one mass, and to have made a fine bobbin, and to have woven from the wool a cloak for the whole populace.

Magistrate: Is it not a disgrace that those who did not even have any part in the war at all should preach to us about flogging and bobbins?

Lysistrata: But we, you utterly accursed man, bear more than twice as much of it as you do, for in the first place we have borne sons and sent them out as soldiers.

Magistrate: Be quiet and don't rake up the past!

Lysistrata: And then when we ought to be cheerful and enjoying our prime, we lie alone in bed because of the military operations that are going on. But never mind our plight! I am worried about the young girls growing old in their rooms.

Magistrate: But don't men also grow old, then?

Lysistrata: Good heavens, it isn't the same thing. For when a man has come back, even though his hair is grey, he soon marries a young girl. But the woman's time is short, and if she doesn't take advantage of it nobody wants to marry her, but she sits trying to tell her fortune, husbandless.

(Aristophanes, Lysistrata 565–597)

THE TRAINING OF A WIFE

The Athenian Xenophon (*c.* 430–*c.* 354 B.C.), a wealthy man who after a military career settled down to a life of hunting and writing in the country, has left amongst his works a tract (*Oeconomicus*) on the management of home and estate. It is in the form of a dialogue between Socrates (whom Xenophon knew and admired) and an Athenian country gentleman Ischomachus (in whom there is clearly more than a little of Xenophon himself).

The training of a wife (important for the smooth running of the household, and Ischomachus is a very fussy person) is discussed— and we should remember that among Mediterranean women today fifteen is not too young an age for marriage. Socrates speaks first:

But this is just what I want to hear from you, Ischomachus, said I. Did you train your wife yourself to be the right kind, or was she instructed in housewifely duties when you received her from her father and mother?

What knowledge could she have had, Socrates, when I took her as my wife? She was not yet fifteen years old when she came to me, and before that she had lived under careful supervision, seeing, hearing and saying as little as possible. If she knew no more when she came than how to turn out a cloak when given the wool, is that not as much as you could expect? For in control of her appetite she had been excellently trained, Socrates; and this kind of training is, in my view, most important to man and woman alike.

But in other respects did you train your wife yourself so that she should be competent to carry out her duties?

Well, Socrates, as soon as I found her docile and domesticated enough to carry on conversation, I questioned her to this effect:

'Tell me, dear, have you realised yet why I took you and your parents gave you to me. For I am sure it is obvious to you that we should have had no difficulty in finding someone else to share our beds. But I on my own behalf and your parents on yours considered who was the best partner for sharing a home and rearing children that we could get. I chose you, and your parents, it seems, chose me as the best they could find. If God allows us to have children, we shall then take thought as to the best form of training for them. For we shall have this blessing in common—the possession of the very best of allies and the very best of support in old age; but at present we share in this our home. For I am putting into the common stock all I have, and you have put in all that you brought with you. And we must not calculate which of us has in fact contributed more, but we should be convinced of this, that the one who is the better partner makes the more valuable contribution.

To this my wife answered, Socrates: 'How could I help you? What power have I? Everything is in your hands, rather. My task, as my mother told me, is to be tactful and discreet.'

'Certainly, dear,' I said, 'my father said the same to me. But discretion in both man and woman means acting in such a manner that their property shall be in the best condition possible, and that as much as possible shall be added to it by fair and just means.'

'And what do you see that I can do to help in the enhancement of our home?' she asked.

'Well,' said I, 'try to do as well as possible what the gods made you able to do and the law allows.'

'And what is that, please?' she said.

'Things, I imagine, of no small account,' I replied, 'unless the tasks over which the queen bee in the hive presides are of small moment. For it seems to me, my dear, that the gods have with great discernment joined together male and female, as they are called, mainly in order that they may form a perfect partnership in service to one another. For in the first place, so that the various kinds of living things may not fail they are joined in wedlock for the begetting of children. Secondly, offspring to provide for them in old age are created by this union (for human beings, at any rate). Thirdly, human beings do not live in the open air, like beasts, but clearly need shelter. Nevertheless, those who intend to gather stores to bring into the shelter need someone who will work at the open-air tasks; for ploughing, sowing, planting and grazing are all such open-air tasks, and these supply the necessary food. Then again, as soon as this is stored in the shelter, there is need of someone to keep it and to work at the jobs that must be done under cover. Cover is needed for the nurture of children; cover is needed for the making of corn into bread, and likewise for the manufacture of clothes from wool. And since both the indoor and the outdoor tasks call for labour and attention, God from the beginning adapted the woman's nature, I think, to the indoor and man's to the outdoor tasks and concerns. ... To the woman, since he has made her body less capable of the necessary endurance for outdoor work, God has assigned the indoor tasks, I take it. And knowing that he had created in the woman and had imposed on her the nourishment of infants, he apportioned to her a larger amount of affection for new-born babies than to man. And God also gave to both impartially the power to practise self-control, and gave authority to whichever is the better (whether it be the man or the woman) to win a larger portion of the good that comes from it. ... To the woman it is more honourable to stay indoors than to stay out of doors, but to the man it is unseemly rather to remain indoors than to attend to work outside. If a man acts contrary to the nature God has given him, perhaps his disobedience is detected by the gods and he receives punishment for neglecting his own work or doing what is really his wife's.' . . .

'Tell me,' said my wife, 'how do the queen bee's tasks resemble those which I have to do?'

'How? She stays in the hive,' I replied, 'and does not allow the bees to be idle; but those whose duty it is to work outside she sends out to their work; and whatever each of them brings in, she knows and receives it, and keeps it safe till it is required for use. And when that time comes, she assigns the just share to each. Similarly, she looks after the weaving of the combs in the hive, seeing that they are well and quickly woven, and cares for the brood of young ones, ensuring that they are duly reared. And when the young bees have been duly reared and are fit for work, she sends them out to found a colony with a leader in charge of the youthful band.'

'Then shall I also have to do these things?' asked my wife.

'Certainly you will,' said I; 'your duty will be to remain indoors and send out those servants whose work lies outside, and superintend those who are to work inside, and to receive what comes in, and distribute so much as must be spent, and keep watch over so much as is to be stored, and see to it that the sum laid by for a year is not spent in a month. And you must see, when the wool is brought to you, that the cloaks are made for those who need them. You must also see that the dry corn is in good condition for making food. One of the tasks that fall to you, however, will perhaps seem rather unpleasant—you will have to see that any sick servant is looked after.'

'Oh no,' my wife exclaimed, 'it will be a very great pleasure —if those who are well cared for are going to feel grateful and be more loyal than before.'

(Xenophon, *Oeconomicus*, 7. 3–37, with omissions)

Ischomachus' lesson continues with comments on the training of women servants in household crafts, from which he passes on to the arrangement of the house itself;—there is to be a place for everything, and everything is to be in its place. He tells his wife about a Phoenician ship he once saw in which all the various pieces of tackle were neatly stowed away and the most made of the narrow space available. That is the pattern for Ischomachus. In relation to his division of labour consider this statement by a modern writer: 'Mechanisation has made the greater physical strength of men become less important in many forms of work, helping women to become as efficient as men over a wider field.'

MEN AND WOMEN EQUAL

Much is heard nowadays about this subject; would you agree that in the debate equality and similarity are often confused? And would you agree that the modern emancipation of women has meant that whilst they have gained many new functions they have lost few of the old ones? Let us now turn to Plato on the question of the equality of the sexes (in the *Republic*):

Do we think that the females of watchdogs should guard as well as the males, and hunt with them, and generally share their activities, or ought they to be kept indoors in the kennels, on the ground that breeding and rearing the puppies renders them unfit for anything else, while the hard work and all the care of the sheep fall to the males?

They ought to share in everything, said Glaucon. Only, we treat the females as the weaker and the males as the stronger.

Is it possible to use any living creature for the same tasks as another unless you give it the same upbringing and training? No.

Then if we make use of women for the same tasks as men we must give them the same instruction?

Yes.

Perhaps if our words are translated into action these proposals may appear to involve many ridiculous breaches of custom.

They certainly will.

Which of them do you see as the most ridiculous? Clearly it is the notion of women exercising naked in the wrestling-school along with men—especially when they are no longer young; and they will present the same sight as the enthusiastic old men who in spite of wrinkles and ugliness devotedly frequent the gymnasia.

Most certainly; according to present notions at least the proposal would seem ridiculous.

But first let us come to an understanding about the nature of woman—is she capable of sharing either wholly or partly in the occupations of men, or not at all? And what of the art of war— is it one of those arts in which she can or cannot share? This would naturally be the best way to begin and lead to the best conclusion.

That will be much the best way.

Shall we take the other side first and start arguing against ourselves? In this way the opposition's case will not lack defence.

Why not?

Let us, then, put words in their mouth: 'Socrates and Glaucon, there is no need for others to find fault with you, for you yourselves, in the beginning of your settlement of the city, admitted the principle that everyone was to do the work suited to his own nature.' And we certainly did make such an admission, if I am not mistaken. 'And do not the natures of men and women differ very much?' And we shall reply: Of course. The next question will be: 'Ought not different tasks to be assigned to men and women in accordance with the nature of each?' Certainly they should. 'Well then, are you not mistaken and inconsistent now in maintaining, as you do, that men and women, whose natures are so entirely different, ought to perform the same actions?'—will you be able to put up any defence to that, my wonderful friend?

(The Platonic reply to this objection—Socrates is still speaking)

Among the various pursuits which belong to the life of the state there is not one that is peculiar to woman as woman or to man as man; natural aptitudes are equally distributed in both; all the pursuits of men are open to women also, but in all of them a woman is inferior to a man. Are we, then, to impose all our enactments upon men and none on women.?

Of course not.

One woman has a gift for healing and another not; one is musical and another is not. One woman has a capacity for gymnastic and military exercises, and another is unwarlike and no lover of gymnastics. One woman is a philosopher, another hates philosophy; one has the spirited temperament, another has not. One woman will be capable of being a guardian or ruler, another not.[1] For was this not the quality for which we looked in our selection of male rulers? Men and women alike have the qualities to make rulers—except that men are naturally stronger and women weaker. And the women who possess such qualities are to be selected to share the life of men of similar character and guard the city along with them, because they are capable and of a kindred nature. The same natures ought to have the same pursuits, and so there is nothing unnatural in assigning a cultural and physical education to the wives of the ruling class, and the law which we made was in accordance with nature and therefore not an impracticable aspiration; and the contrary practice which prevails today is much more evidently a departure from nature. We must, then, make the wives of our rulers strip, for their virtue will be their dress, and we must make them take their share in war and the other duties of guarding the city;— only, in the distribution of duties the lighter are to be assigned to the women as being the weaker sex.

(Plato, *Republic* 451d–457b, with omissions)

THE STOIC VIEW OF SEXUAL EQUALITY

Preaching the brotherhood of man, Stoicism urged that no distinction was to be made between Greek and barbarian, Roman and stranger, male and female, bond and free (see p. 21). Seneca, writing to console Marcia, a Roman lady who had lost a son, touches upon this doctrine;

---

[1] The reference is to the three kinds of temperament postulated by Plato (see p. 13 and pp. 68 ff.): the 'philosophic' or reflective which produces thinkers, artists and statesmen; the 'spirited' which is fearless and pugnacious and produces soldiers; and the 'appetitive' which puts money and pleasure above all else. The threefold division of the populace in Plato's ideal commonwealth is based on this classification.

Stoicism denied the common assumption about the moral and intellectual inferiority of women.

I know what you are saying: 'You have forgotten that it is a woman you are consoling; the examples you give refer to men.' But who has asserted that nature has dealt meanly with women's natures and has restricted their virtue narrowly? They have, believe me, just as much force and just as much capacity, if they like, for virtuous conduct; they are just as able to bear pain and suffering once they are used to them.

(Seneca, *ad Marciam* 16.1)

THE ROMAN MATRON

The Roman father's authority over the persons and goods of wife, sons, unmarried daughters, clients (free men who entrusted themselves to him and received his protection) and slaves was in law absolute. In this assertion of paternal authority the Roman family was unique when compared with the same institution in other ancient societies and in modern times. A Roman woman of free citizen birth was either in the power (*potestas*) of her father or, after marriage, of her husband or, in widowhood, under the guardianship of a male relative. But legal theory was in practice modified at most points, and by the force of custom the Roman matron had secured to her a degree of dignity and respect generally unknown to mothers elsewhere. A progressive relaxation in social attitudes at Rome had by the middle of the first century B.C. accorded women a freedom and independence almost unparalleled anywhere till our own day. But the ancestral ideal of loyalty to family obligations (*pietas*—see p. 23) long remained a living force amongst Romans.

Consider now this Roman funerary inscription which dates from somewhere about 140 B.C. It commemorates the virtues of a Roman wife and mother, and in its simple dignity is very touching. Perhaps her husband composed it.

Stranger, I have but little to say; stop and read. Here stands the scarcely lovely tomb of a lovely lady. Her parents gave her the name Claudia. She loved her husband from the bottom of her heart. She gave birth to two sons. One of these she left alive on earth, the other she had buried beneath the earth. She was a

lady of charming talk, and of graceful movements besides. She
was a home-keeping person. She spun and wove her wool.
I have finished. Go on your way!

(Bücheler, *Carmina Epigraphica* 52)

We now turn to some extracts from a funeral elegy by the Roman
love poet Propertius who wrote during the second half of the first
century B.C. It is on a well-born lady Cornelia whose husband
Paullus had held high office in the state, and is in the form of a
monologue spoken by the dead woman, a common device in monu-
mental epigrams (cp. the last piece on Claudia). She addresses first
the judges of the dead and then her family. The poem is redolent of
the Roman domestic virtues and with its deep note of sincerity it is
perhaps the poet's greatest work.

Cease, Paullus, to besiege my tomb with tears; no prayers
unlock the black gate. When once the dead have become subject to the rule of Hell the ways of escape are fast barred with
unyielding rock. Though your prayer may be heard by the god
of the dark hall, the shores of the river Styx[1] will drink up your
tears unmoved. Olympian gods respond to vows, but once the
ferryman has received his fee, the ghastly gate closes on the
world of shadows. So sang the mournful trumpets when the
cruel torch was placed beneath my pyre and the flames
sapped my substance.

Marriage with Paullus, the triumphs of ancestors, children,
firm pledges of my fame—what help were these to me? Cornelia did not find the Fates less cruel for all this, and now I am
just one small handful of dust. . . .

When I had put aside my childhood dress before the marriage torch and had caught up and bound my hair with a new
fillet, I was wedded to your couch, Paullus, doomed alas! to
leave you so soon. On this stone will be read these words:
'She was the wife of one man.' . . .

I have not swerved from the path, my life has been blame-
less. Between the two torches of marriage and death ours was a

---

[1] Styx—a river of the Underworld, over which Charon the ferryman
rowed the dead.

life of great renown. The laws I followed were taught me by my heredity—my obedience did not spring from fear of a judge. . . .

Nor, sweet mother, Scribonia, have I wronged you. Except for my early death, what would you have changed in me? My mother's tears and the laments of Rome honour me, and my ashes find support in the grief of Caesar;—Caesar moaning cries that in me his daughter had a worthy sister, and we have thus seen that even a god may weep.[1]

I achieved the maternal robe of honour, having borne three children; it was from no unfruitful home that death snatched me. Lepidus and Paullus, even now you bring me comfort. It was your arms that supported me when I closed my eyes at the last. Twice I saw my brother also sit in the chair of high office, and at the very hour they chose him consul[2] I his sister was snatched away. And you, my daughter, born to reflect your father's high virtue, see that you follow my example and wed one man and one man only. Children, see that you perpetuate the family name. I am not hesitant to put out in the boat of death since so many of my blood will add fresh lustre to my deeds. A woman's greatest triumph is when free comment round her pyre sings her praises.

And now to you, Paullus, I commend your children, the common pledges of our love; concern for them still lives, burned deeply even into my ashes. You, the father, must fill the place of a mother; the whole weight of the family must rest on your shoulders. When you kiss their tears away, kiss them too for me; from now on the whole house must be your burden. If you must shed tears, do so when they are not present; deceive their kisses with dry eyes. Let the nights which you wear out in thoughts of me be enough for you, Paullus, and the dreams in which you often imagine you see me myself; and

---

[1] Caesar—the Emperor Augustus (63 B.C.—A.D. 14) whose daughter Julia was half-sister to Cornelia. Augustus and his successors were officially regarded as divine after death and occasionally, as here, even before it.

[2] P. Cornelius Scipio, Cornelia's brother, was consul in 16 B.C. On her father's side Cornelia was descended from Scipio Africanus the younger, who conquered Carthage, and on her mother's side from the Libones, a Roman aristocratic clan.

when in secret you speak to my portrait utter every word as though to one who will reply.

Yet, if another bed should stand facing the door and a step-mother, on her guard, takes my place, praise and bear with your father's choice, my sons; by good manners you will win her over. And do not praise your mother overmuch, for she will take offence if compared too freely with her predecessor. But if your father does not forget me, if my shade is enough for him and he still shows affection for my ashes, watch tenderly for the first signs of age in him and do all you can to keep him free from unhappiness in his wifeless state. May the years that were taken from me be added to yours; thus may my children's presence bring comfort to Paullus in his old age. This is as it should be;—I never wore mourning for any child of mine; all my children came to my funeral.

My speech is ended; rise up, you who mourn for me, and as witnesses support my plea, and wait for earth's kindly verdict which shall give the reward my life has earned. Even heaven sometimes opens its gates to worth—may I be found deserving, and may my ashes be borne to dwell with my glorious ancestors.

(Propertius 4.11, with omissions)

We close now with a charming sketch of tranquil marital content-ment, all the more remarkable for being the work of Ovid (Publius Ovidius Naso, 43 B.C.–A.D. 17?) who had made his reputation as a poet of light love. The simple countrywoman Baucis and her husband Philemon entertained unawares Zeus and Hermes who had been refused hospitality elsewhere.

Good old Baucis and Philemon, of equal age, were in that cottage wedded in their youth, and in that cottage had grown old together. There they made light of their poverty by acknowledging it and by bearing it with a contented spirit. There was no point in asking for master or servants in that house—the two of them formed the whole household, together they both served and gave orders. And so when the heavenly deities came to this humble home and, stooping, entered at the low door, the old man placed a bench and told them to rest their limbs, while over this bench busy Baucis threw a rough cover. Then she raked aside the warm ashes on the hearth and fanned yesterday's coal into life, feeding it with leaves and dry bark and blowing it into flame with the breath of her old body. Next she took down from the roof some fine-split wood and dry twigs, broke them up and placed them under the little copper kettle. And she took the cabbage which her husband had brought in from the well-watered garden and cut off its outside leaves. Meanwhile the old man with a forked stick lifted down a chine of smoked bacon which was hanging from a blackened beam and, having cut off a small piece from the long preserved pork, he set it to cook in the boiling water. . . . The old woman, with her skirts tucked up, set out the table with trembling hands, but one of its three legs was too short and so she propped it up with a tile. . . . Here were nuts and figs, with dried dates, plums and fragrant apples in wide baskets, and purple grapes just picked from the vines; in the centre of the table was a comb of clear white honey. In addition to all this, kindly faces were at the table and lively and plentiful goodwill.

(Ovid, *Metamorphoses* 8. 630–678, with
omissions)

Index of Passages

Index of Subjects